~ATE DUE

SERIOUS
TALK

SERIOUS TALK

Science AND Religion
IN DIALOGUE

John Polkinghorne

TRINITY PRESS INTERNATIONAL
Harrisburg, Pennsylvania

Trinity Press International, P.O. Box 1321, Harrisburg, PA 17105
Trinity Press International is a division of The Morehouse Group.

Library of Congress Cataloging-in-Publication Data

Polkinghorne, J. C., 1930–
    Serious talk : science and religion in dialogue / John Polkinghorne.
        p. cm.
    Includes bibliographical references and index.
    ISBN 1-56338-109-5 (pa)
    1. Religion and science. 2. Creation. 3. Providence and government of God. 4. Jesus Christ—Resurrection. 5. Eschatology. I. Title.
BL240.2.P5764   1995
261.5'5–dc20   95-6976
                                                                            CIP

Printed in the United States of America

98   99   00   01   02   03   10   9   8   7   6   5   4   3   2

CONTENTS

PREFACE

ALTHOUGH I AM NOW an Anglican priest and also head of one of the colleges of Cambridge University, I have spent most of my adult life working as a theoretical physicist. I have always thought that the habits of thought so natural to a scientist are ones that can be followed also in the search for a wider and deeper kind of truth about the world. They include what I sometimes call "bottom-up" thinking; that is to say, starting, not with grand general principles, but with the particularity of experience and then asking what is sufficient to explain the phenomena and give an understanding of what is going on. I approach my Christian faith in this way, and that is why I feel that it is not threatened by my living in an age of great scientific advance (chapter 1).

If the study of science teaches one anything, it is that the world is full of surprises — that reality is stranger (and much more interesting) than we could have imagined. Who would have supposed that the clear and reliable world of everyday experience is made of subatomic constituents whose behavior is cloudy and fitful? Quantum theory has greatly changed our ideas of the nature of the physical world and liberated us from a rigidly mechanical conception of reality. I used quantum theory everyday in my working life as a theoretical physicist, as did thousands of my colleagues. Invented to describe atoms, it is now applied with great success to account for the behavior of quarks and gluons, which are at least a hundred million times smaller than atoms. Yet a great paradox remains. We still do not understand quantum theory fully. The measurement problem (how the fitful quantum world and the reliable everyday world interlock) is still a matter of unresolved dispute (chapter 2).

It is a common theme among many of us who want to take science and theology seriously that, despite the great differences of their subject matter, the two disciplines are in many ways intellectual cousins as they pursue the search for motivated belief. I believe I can identify eight parallel characteristics of each subject through which their kinship is clearly displayed (chapters 3 and 4).

The first half of this book (corresponding to my lectures at the University of Waterloo) seeks to establish a comradely meeting point for science and religion. The second half (corresponding to my lectures and sermon at the Memorial Church, Harvard University) is concerned with looking at some specific theological issues approached in the spirit of such an encounter. The first topic is creation. Science tells us how cosmic history started and how it has progressed; theology is concerned with asserting that there has been a mind and purpose behind that process. Two different kinds of issue are involved for science and religion respectively (in simple terms, How? and Why?), which therefore cannot be in conflict with each other. I do not have to make a choice between them. I can believe (as I do) in the Big Bang and in God the Creator. Yet, if I am to hold those beliefs together with integrity, there must be some fitting relationship of consonance between them. I believe that there is. The intellectual beauty of the order discovered by science is consistent with the physical world's having behind it the mind of the divine Creator; the insight of the anthropic principle into the finely tuned balance built into the laws determining the very physical fabric of the universe is consistent with its fruitful history being the expression of divine purpose. The role of chance (happenstance) is the consequence of the Creator's gift of a genuine independence to creation (chapter 5).

If God is personal, then divine action must be more particular than simply a general upholding of the world in being. The death of mere mechanism, signaled by the twentieth-century sciences of quantum theory and chaos theory, affords the opportunity for a metaphysical account of a universe open to both human and divine agency. Such a supple and subtle world is one of true becoming and one in which a scientist can pray. For theology, this implies that the eternal God has also a true engagement with time (chapter 6).

At the heart of Christian belief is the stupendous claim of Christ's resurrection. Such a belief must be motivated. I seek to exhibit and evaluate the historical evidence, concluding that there are good grounds for this Christian claim. The miracle of the resurrection also makes sense as the sign of a deeper insight into the nature of God than is afforded by everyday religious experience, and as the anticipation of a destiny awaiting all humanity beyond death (chapter 7).

Ultimately, the universe will end badly in either collapse or decay. Christians believe that this will not frustrate the Creator's purpose but that God will redeem the universe together with humanity. Despite the mystery of such a destiny, I believe that it is a coherent hope that all shall in the end be well (chapter 8).

It was a privilege and an honor for me to give the Pascal Lectures at the University of Waterloo and the William Belden Noble Lectures at Harvard University. I thank those involved in extending the invitations and in the provision of generous hospitality. In particular, I am most grateful to Mrs. Joan Hadley, Dr. Robert Mann, Professor Peter Gomes, and Dr. Krister Sairsingh for their personal kindnesses to me.

The material of chapters 3 and 4 was also the basis of my Idreos Lectures at Manchester College, Oxford. I am grateful to Rev. Dr. Ralph Waller for kind hospitality.

– One –

CHRISTIAN BELIEF
IN A SCIENTIFIC AGE

H OW DOES SOMEBODY like myself, and perhaps many of
you, whose habits of thought — for good or ill — have
been formed by modern science, encounter questions of Christian belief? That is a big question, and obviously I cannot do
more than sketch an answer to it.

As a scientist, my thought is conditioned by two things.
First, I am naturally a "bottom-up" thinker rather than a "top-
down" thinker. By that I mean that my instinct is to start with
a phenomenon, something I am trying to understand and explain, and then to build up from that, rather than starting
with some broad, general principles and working downward
from them.

I am very convinced of the unity of knowledge. There is one
world of human experience and human understanding that we
are trying to come to grips with. If we are to understand that
world, we need the insights both of science and of religion,
and of a number of other forms of rational human inquiry
as well. Therefore, I see science and religion as being complementary and not conflicting. So for me, religion, or religious
understanding, is part of a general, rational inquiry into the
nature of reality. Faith is motivated belief. Faith is not a ques-

tion of shutting our eyes and gritting our teeth and believing
five impossible things before breakfast. It is a leap, but a leap
into the light and not a leap into the dark. In that sense, it is
like scientific belief, which is also motivated by our experience
of the world. But religious belief is different from scientific belief in the sense that religion involves us as whole people, and
therefore it has consequences not only for what we understand
but also for how we behave. It involves practice and obedience
as well as understanding. In that sense, religious belief is more
like moral belief than scientific belief. Also, religious belief is
concerned with that realm of personal encounter in which the
way we know things is conditioned by the nature of the things
that we are seeking to know. We know that in science itself. We
know the elusive, fitful quantum world in a way different from
the way we know the reliable world of everyday physics. We
know them in different ways because they have different na-
tures. All our encounters with reality are conditioned by the
nature of the reality with which we are in contact. In science,
we are in contact with the physical world treated as an object,
treated as an "it," open to us to manipulate through the marvelous resource of the experimental method. I was a theoretical
physicist myself, but I would gladly testify to the central importance of the experimental method. Science can put things to
the test because it is concerned with an impersonal encounter
with the world. But religion is part of a broad spectrum of personal encounter with reality. In that domain of our experience,
testing has to give way to trusting. We know that is so in our relationships with each other. If I were always setting little traps
to see if you were my friend, by these very acts I would destroy
the possibility of friendship between us. And this is true, not
only of our relationship with each other, but also of our relationship with God. God is not to be put to the test in that sort
of way. Our knowledge of God is of a different character.

My instinct as a scientist is not to ask, Is something reasonable? but rather, What reason do we have to think it might be
the case? We know the physical world is very surprising, and

we cannot guess beforehand what it is going to be like. Who would have guessed quantum theory beforehand? The answer is nobody! Similarly, in our encounter with God, we must expect surprises. In a search for motivated belief, we ask: What is the evidence?, What are the things that might make us think this was the case? I am also looking for a unified explanation, a unified understanding; one world and one truth is what I am looking for. The theological quest is the ultimate search for a Grand Unified Theory — a GUT, as we say in physics.

I will make some broad points and will then discuss some of the difficulties and perplexities that I see in Christian belief.

First, we are looking for one truth about one world. We are looking, therefore, for some form of total explanation and total understanding of the world. When we look for that, there are really two possible starting points. Everybody who is seeking an understanding of the world must have some given assumption as the basic starting point. Nothing comes of nothing. If we are to understand things, we must have some basic beliefs, some intellectual commitment, in terms of which our explanation will be framed. If we are to understand the nature of reality, we have only two possible starting points: either the brute fact of the physical world or the brute fact of a divine will and purpose behind that physical world. These are the only two intellectually respectable starting points, as we push the argument back; therefore here are the only two possible foundation points as we then draw the argument forward. Someone like the Scottish skeptic David Hume would say, "Just start with brute matter, the fact of the physical world. You don't need more than that." That would be a materialist answer to the problem. Why should one go back beyond that to look for the will of a divine agent, a creatorly purpose at work in the world? The question where you start or stop is a question of where you feel intellectually comfortable — were you feel you have a basic belief that is not begging important questions.

Impressive though our scientific understanding of the world is, and impressive as our grasp of the laws of nature is, the laws of nature are not by themselves sufficiently intellectually satisfying, sufficiently self-explanatory to be an adequate and acceptable foundation on which to build one truth about one world. I say that because if we take physics seriously, we see that there are inescapable questions that seem to arise from the laws of nature, questions that seem sensible to ask but that push us beyond taking those laws as our unexplained starting point.

Two meta-questions (questions going beyond) arise from the laws of science and seem to indicate that they are not themselves a comfortable intellectual resting place.

One is our amazing power to understand the physical world — the fact that the physical world is rationally transparent to us to a quite astonishing degree, and that in that transparency it is mathematics which plays the key role. It is an actual technique in fundamental physics, which has proved its worth and fruitfulness time and again in the history of physics, to seek for theories that in their mathematical expression are economic and elegant, in the expectation that it is such theories that explain what is going on in the physical world. When we use mathematics in that sort of way something very odd is happening. Why does our reason so perfectly fit the physical world? One might say, "Otherwise we wouldn't have survived in the struggle for existence." That is true up to a point. But it is true only of our everyday experience and our everyday thinking about that experience. When I point to the marvelous power of mathematics to illuminate our understanding of the physical world, for example, I am referring to the quantum world, which is totally counterintuitive, totally unpicturable in everyday terms; but is not unintelligible to us, though its understanding requires in fact very abstract forms of mathematics. So it does seem that there is something to understand — why the world is so intelligible, why science is possible. Not only does it strike me that way, but it also struck Einstein, which is perhaps a rather more impressive thing to say. He once said, "The only incomprehensible thing about the universe is that it is comprehensible." So, I would like to understand why the world is so rationally transparent. An explanation would be that the physical world is shot through with signs of mind because behind it is in fact the mind of the Creator. The rational beauty of the world depends upon the creative and purposive mind that has brought it into being. That might be one way of understanding it.

I would now draw your attention to another aspect of the laws of nature that for me does not make them sufficiently self-explanatory to be a comfortable, intellectual resting place. It is the amazing insight that the astonishing fruitfulness of the physical world is because of a very special fine-tuning in the laws of nature that govern that physical world. We all know that the world as we know it originated about 15 billion years ago in the fiery explosion of the "Big Bang." It started very simply. It was just a uniform ball of energy. One of the reasons cosmologists can talk with such great bravado about the very early universe is that the very early universe was very simple and therefore is very easy to think about. But the world that was so simple has become very complicated to include within it such amazing consequences as you and me, who have emerged during the 15-billion-year evolving history. Now our understanding of it is that it is only in a world that is very, very particular, very special, that such fruitfulness is possible. If you were to change the laws of nature a little bit, if you made gravity a little bit stronger or electromagnetism a little bit weaker, or if you fiddled around with nuclear forces in some way — things that you would have thought would not have had really significant effects upon cosmic history — you would find, in fact, that those small changes would have made the history of the universe boring and sterile. We live in a world in a trillion. What do we make of that?

One of the people who has thought about that quite a bit is John Leslie, of the University of Guelph. John does philosophy by telling stories. He is a sort of parabolic philosopher. John tells the following story: You are about to be executed, and ten sharpshooters are lined up with their rifles trained on you. The shots ring out, and to your amazement you find that you are still alive. Now, that is a very remarkable fact — so remarkable a fact that it requires an explanation. It is not rational just to shrug your shoulders and say, "Well, gee, that's the way it is. I just happened to survive." You want to know *why* it happened. Similarly, he suggests, when you look at the fine-tuning of the universe it is not enough to say, "We're here because were here; it just happens to be that way!" It is rational to ask why it is so. Going back to the execution, Leslie says there are only two rational explanations. One is that there were many executions taking place that day, and you happened to be the lucky one in which all the sharpshooters missed. That is one explanation. The other explanation is that the sharpshooters were on your side. There was more going on than met the eye.

Those two explanations, translated back into the world of the anthropic principle (which is what "fine-tuning" is called by the learned) suggests that the remarkable, fruitful, specialness of the fine-tuning of the universe has two possible explanations. Maybe there are lots and lots of different universes. And if there are, then it is not very surprising if one of them happens to have the particular physical laws and circumstances that make you and me possible. That is the one in which we live, because we could not appear anywhere else. This is the "many executions" solution to the problem; translated, it becomes the "many universes" solution of anthropic significance. The other, of course, is that there is only one universe — there is only one execution — but the sharpshooters are on our side. In other words, there is a purpose behind the fruitful fine-tuning of the universe.

The choice between the two explanations is a choice not between a scientific explanation and a religious explanation, but two alternative metaphysical explanations. Science speaks only of one universe of our own experience. People try to trick out a "many universe" account in sort of pseudo-scientific terms, but that is pseudo-science. It is a metaphysical guess that there might be many universes with different laws and circumstances.

I am not against metaphysics. In fact, we cannot live without it, whether we know it or not. But an alternative metaphysical guess is that there is one universe, which is a creation whose fine-tuning is the expression of the fruitful will of its Creator. That is to me a more economic and elegant metaphysical conjecture than the "many universes" one.

I have given two arguments, derived from science but pointing beyond science, both of which are capable of satisfying interpretation in a religious sense. I do not present either of these insights as knockdown arguments. I am not saying, because the universe is intelligible, God exists. Or, because our existence requires fine-tuning of the laws of nature, God exists. I do not think there are any knockdown arguments of that sort, either for God's existence or for God's nonexistence. But I do present them as intellectually satisfying and coherent insights. And if we believe that there are other reasons for believing in God's existence, they become also economic explanations of what is going on. Science, even by itself, points beyond itself in ways that are certainly capable of a religious interpretation.

I will now discuss other arguments that again are a bottom-up look at the phenomena, arguments that encourage in me a religious belief. I will be assembling some sort of cumulative case for the existence of God.

Another strand of phenomena that I want to look at is the amazing, richly structured, many-leveled character of our experience. Science is successful partly by the modesty of its ambitions, by its self-limitation. It looks only at certain aspects of the world around us. That world is in fact experienced and understood in terms of many different coexisting levels. For example, consider music. From the point of view of science, music is just vibrations in the air and that is all. You can Fourier-analyze those vibrations into their component frequencies. In that way, someone knowledgeable in acoustics would give a complete scientific description of, for example, Bach's Mass in B Minor. But we know that Bach's Mass in B Minor is more than just a collection of vibrations in the air. It is some-

thing that speaks to us very deeply, and I think very truly. I
take utterly seriously our experiences of beauty. I think they
tell something about reality. Beauty is not just a sort of froth
on the surface of things. It is something very deep about the
world. So how am I to understand the remarkable fact that the
physical world is also the carrier of beauty? That is what I mean
by many-leveled structure; there is in the world beauty as well
as physics.

The world is not only the carrier of beauty; it is also the
arena of moral choice. And I believe that we know some things
ethically and quite certainly. I believe that I know that torturing
children is wrong as surely as I know anything. I know some an-
thropologists will pop up and tell me lots of interesting things
that I must take seriously about ethical relativism between different cultural communities, but when I have taken all that into
account, there is still, for me, an irreducible ethical element in
the world that is again an experience of reality. And where does
it come from? That is another level. And I would add a further
level, the level of religious experience, of encounter with God
and the experience of worship — a very, very widespread experience through both space and time. Not all of us perhaps
feel that we have had that experience; some of us may deny
its existence. But for me, I cannot deny its existence. My own
experience of encounter through worship, with a Reality stand-
ing over against me in mercy and in judgment, however faint
and fitful those encounters are, is undeniable experience for me.
These encounters are phenomena that I must take into account.

So we have this richly structured world in which we live.
But how does it come about that the world is perceived and
experienced in all these different ways — the one world of our
experience? An attraction of religious belief is that it ties together all those forms of experience. I have already suggested
that the rational order of the world that science discerns so
successfully is an intimation of the reasoned will of the Creator behind the world. I also believe that our experiences of
beauty are sharing in God's joy in creation, that our intima-

tions of ethics are intuitions of the divine will and purpose for the world, and that our experiences of worship are encounters with that divine reality. So there is a sort of cumulative tying together, a synthetic power in religious belief that makes connections between these different levels of human experiences that would be difficult to make any other way. That is a line of argument that persuades me to take religion seriously and to look for a religious belief in a scientific age. Science is great, but it is not enough by any manner of means. There are aspects of reality that we have to take with equal or greater seriousness and that, somehow or other, we must incorporate into this one truth about the one world in which we live. For me, religious belief helps me to do that.

Well, so far so good, or so far so bad if you do not follow me in the argument. The arguments thus far have been fairly general, but I am really talking about Christian belief in a scientific age. I am doing that because I am myself a Christian believer and, indeed, a Christian priest, so it is about time I said something about the specifically Christian aspects of religious belief.

I have to say that I am greatly moved by the figure of Christ. I seek to understand that figure, and I seek to do that by looking at the record of his life that we find set before us in the Gospels. When I read the Gospels I want to read them as evidence. I want to submit them to some form of critical assessment. I do not believe that they are divinely guaranteed documents that I must not question in any sort of way. I need to look at them and see them as historical sources and see that they are already interpreted accounts of experience. We always interpret experience, just as every scientific experiment is an interpreted experience. There are no uninterpreted experiments; every experiment is theory laden. The Gospels are themselves also theory laden in their way. I must take that into account in assessing what they have to say.

When I look at the Gospels, there are three striking factors. First, there is this extremely captivating but also extremely mysterious figure who is presented to us. Jesus is a person whose words contained tremendous hope and promise, and whose deeds seemed to carry that out. However, he was also strange and upsetting in various ways. He said awful things like "let the dead bury their dead — a very shocking thing to say. He also said, "If you want to follow me, take up your cross," not meaning some pleasing, precious-metal, ecclesiastical symbol, but, "take up the gallows of execution, carry the cross beam for your execution with you." These are very strange and disturbing things to say. But there is a commanding power about Jesus. So somehow or other, in my account of reality, I must reckon with him. I am not taking account of the phenomena adequately if I do not take account of the phenomenon of Christ.

Second, the most astonishing thing about the story of Jesus is the end of the story. Almost all the other great world's religious leaders die in honored old age. That is true of Moses; it is true of the Buddha; it is true of Muhammad. But Jesus does not die that way. He dies in middle life; he dies a miserable failure; he dies a deserted death. The story of the disciples fleeing, of Peter denying Christ — a story that is found in all four Gospels — must be true. Such a story would not have been recorded about a powerful figure in the early church unless it were true. Jesus dies a felon's death — not only a felon's death, but a death that pious Jews viewed with the greatest abhorrence because of a verse in Deuteronomy that says, "Cursed is he who hangs on a tree." So Jesus dies in the darkness and dereliction of Calvary, and he dies with that terrible cry on his lips — again recorded in two of the Gospels, which says something about the integrity of the Gospel writers — "My God, my God. Why hast thou forsaken me?" The one who in his lifetime had so consistently proclaimed the fatherhood of God and encouraged trust in the One who looks after the lilies and the ravens dies in that miserable way and dies with that strange and terrible cry on his lips. There is something tremendously peculiar in the death of Christ. Now what do we see in that lonely figure? There are all sorts of possibilities. We might see just a good man who, like many good men both before and after him, has been caught and broken by the system. Or we might see a megalomaniac who had made plans for himself that went beyond what was decent or sensible for a human to do and who got his comeuppance. That might be another understanding. However, it has been the consistent claim, from the very earliest days of the church and of his followers today, that we see neither of those things. Rather, we see one whose death is in fact the source of life. We see hanging in the darkness of Calvary the Savior of the world. There is this great ambiguity in the death of Christ. It is an ambiguity that can be answered, not by human conjecture, but only by some sort of divine response. It is Christian belief that God did provide that answer by raising Jesus from the dead on the first Easter day.

The third thing I want to say about Jesus is that I believe that that indeed is what happened; I believe that God raised Christ from the dead that first Easter day. Of course, that is a very bold and astonishing assertion to make and I could easily explain at length why I think that is a motivated belief. It is a belief that can be neither proved nor disproved. But it is a motivated belief for me. All I can do is say why I think such a astonishing thing actually happened.

What happened on that day was something really rather remarkable, because on Good Friday we see the disciples demoralized, all their hopes completely shattered in a very obvious and understandable way. But it is equally clear that within a very short time those same disciples who fled from the authorities are popping up again in Jerusalem and are claiming that this Jesus, who had been executed a few weeks earlier, is God's Lord and Christ — that is, God's Anointed One, God's Chosen One for fulfilling his purpose. And they are defying the authorities in ways that eventually lead to the death of many of them. That is a very, very big change in a very short time, and *something* must have happened to bring it about. I do not think it can be anything as simple as just taking thought and thinking, "Well, we must say the cause of Jesus carries on even if he did die a rather miserable death." Something much more tremendous and much more transforming must have happened to bring it about. There are accounts in the Gospels that claim to tell us what happened — that in fact Jesus' tomb was found to be empty and that Jesus appeared alive to various people after his death. What are we to make of such stories? Again, that requires careful, patient, sifting analysis.

The stories of the empty tomb occur in all the Gospels. There are many different details among the stories, for example, regarding the timing and how many women went to the tomb. There are variations, but not variations that would astonish anyone who has ever listened to evidence in a police court. They all have in common the discovery to the empty tomb. This key discovery was made by women. For made-up stories in the first century, that is a very odd thing to make up. In that world, women were in a subordinate position, and women's evidence was not allowed to be taken in court. If one were to make up a story, one would not likely make the women the first witnesses.

Then there are those stories about people who met Jesus. They are very different in all the Gospels. They are slightly perplexing stories in some ways, but there is something again about them that persuades me that they are reminiscences. In almost all the stories there is a very unexpected motif that pops up in different ways; that is, how difficult it was to recognize Jesus. There are the two persons walking to Emmaus, when someone joins them whom they do not recognize. In John's Gospel, the disciples are fishing when a figure appears on the shore. Only one disciple has the insight to make out that it is Jesus. These stories exemplify this recurrent motif, of the difficulty in recognizing Jesus. This motif is a very odd thing to put into stories that are made up, and it is a very odd motif to recur in stories that are so different in character from each other. I am myself persuaded that these are actual historical reminiscences. I am persuaded that behind these stories lie actual historical reminiscence of encounters with the risen Christ.

There is much more one could say, but I must leave it there.

I am persuaded, however, that in Christ something tremendous happened. I am led ultimately to the most astonishing Christian idea. Christian thought is based upon the most exciting notion that the unimaginable and unseen God has acted to make himself known by actually living the life of a man; God has made himself known in human terms. That is a very, very exciting idea. I also happen to believe it is true. Not every exciting idea is true, but I believe that this one is. I am trying to offer just a flavor of what it means to have Christian belief in a scientific age to be a bottom-up thinker, seeking motivated belief, wanting to look at the phenomena — not accepting things because the Bible tells me so, or the pope tells me so, but because I have derived them from looking at the evidence.

There must be some difficulties and perplexities. Well, there are, of course. I want briefly to mention three. The most difficult problem that holds more people back from religious belief than anything else, one that is a perpetual problem for those of us who stand within the community of religious belief, is the problem of suffering. Does this world look like the creation of an almighty and loving God? The frank answer is, not at first sight. It seems a world of strange bitterness. There are various philosophical answers that one could make. There is the free-will defense in relation to moral evil; that the ills and cruelties of humankind are the necessary costs for having been endowed with free choice, and that free choice is a morally desirable property. There is what I call a free-process defense in relation to physical evil; that God allows the world to be itself and does not stop tectonic plates from slipping and producing an earthquake, because they are allowed to be themselves just as we are allowed to be ourselves. All those things are moderately helpful, but they do not touch the depth of the problem. I would not want to suggest that there is any facile answer to the problem of suffering. But there is a particular Christian answer that is very important to me, one that is really central to my own Christian belief. It is this: the Christian God is not a benevolent spectator looking down upon the suffering of this strange and bitter world; rather the Christian God is a fellow participant who knows suffering from the inside. The Christian God is the crucified God. We believe that in that figure hanging in the darkness and dereliction of Calvary we see God in human terms opening his arms to embrace the bitterness of the world and to be impaled upon its contradiction. That is an extremely powerful and deep thought; it is for me the makings of the Christian answer to the problem of suffering.

The second difficulty is the question of miracles. I have already spoken about the resurrection, and I think that the resurrection is central to Christian belief. Can we really believe it? Surely the one thing we have learned from science is that the world is very regular and reliable. Dead men just stay dead; how can there be one exception to that in the course of history? I must offer a brief reply. The problem of miracle is actually not a scientific problem because science does not speak about such events. It is a theological problem. And the theological problem of miracle is this: How can God, who must be totally consistent, do utterly unexpected and unprecedented things? The one thing that is theologically quite incredible is that God is some sort of celestial conjurer who does a trick today, which, he did not think of doing yesterday and will not be bothered to do tomorrow. God must be utterly consistent. That is the problem of miracle, and that is what I have to wrestle with when I think about miracles, when I think about the resurrection. Now, consistency is not the same as dreary uniformity. God must be consistent, but in different circumstances. God can do different things. We are very familiar with that from science. The laws of nature do not change, but the consequences of the laws of nature change very drastically. When, for example, we cool a metal down below the critical temperature, it can change from a conductive regime to a superconductive regime. In one regime the laws of nature mean that there is a resistance, and one must have a battery to drive the current round. In the other regime there is no resistance, and the current just circulates without a battery. That is a very radical change. It must have absolutely astonished Kammerlingh Onnes in 1911 when he discovered it. But the laws of physics do not change at the critical point; they just happen to have different consequences in different regimes. So when I try to think about miracles and when I think about the resurrection of Christ, I try to follow that line of thought. If it is true that God is in Christ in that special way that I described, then Jesus does represent a special regime, and it is at least a coherent possibility that that new regime should be accompanied by new phenomena. Also, I believe that Jesus' resurrection within history is an anticipation of a universal human destiny beyond history. "As in Adam all die, even so in Christ shall all be made alive," is how Paul put it.

The third difficulty I must mention for honesty's sake. I have been speaking of Christianity, and quite a lot of what I have said, until 1 started talking about Christ, would be common also to a Jewish or an Islamic view of the world. But we are very conscious of the existence of the world's different religious traditions. Islam and Judaism evaluate Jesus very differently than I do, just as the Far Eastern religions evaluate the physical world in ways very different from those of the religions of the Near East. There is great variation among the world's different religious traditions. They are speaking about some common domain of spiritual experience, but they speak about it in very different ways. They do not just all say the same thing in a different language; they are saying *different* things. What is the nature of time? Is it a path to be trodden or a wheel from which to seek release? It seems to me that there is a conflict here. I am perplexed by that, and I am perplexed by the contrast with science. If you stop people in the street in Toronto or Delhi or Tokyo and ask them what matter is made of, they will say quarks and gluons — if you stop the right persons! If you stop persons in the streets in those cities and ask what is the nature of Ultimate Reality, the chances are you will get different answers. I am puzzled by that. Clearly, cultural effects come in, but that does not seem the whole story. I do not really know why the world's religious traditions are so different from each other. I just have to confess my perplexity here.

In summary, I really do believe in the search for truth and the search for a unified truth — one truth about one world. I also believe, and this is a Christian tradition, that those who are truly seeking understanding, who are truly seeking the truth and are open to it, are seeking God whether they name God by name or not. I believe that Christian belief is possible in a scientific age precisely because it is the search for truth, and science is one, but only one component, and in many ways quite a humble component, in that search for truth.

One of my favorite quotations is from a Canadian Jesuit, Bernard Lonergan, who died a few years ago. He said this: "God is the unrestricted act of understanding, the eternal rapture glimpsed in every Archimedean cry of Eureka."[1]

– Two –

UNDERSTANDING QUANTUM THEORY

E VERYONE KNOWS that quantum theory is a paradoxical sort of subject, but the greatest paradox of quantum theory sometimes escapes people's attention. Quantum theory in its modern form came into being during 1925–26. It was invented in order to describe the behavior of atoms, and it has proved consistently successful in all its applications since then. We use it now to think about the behavior of quarks and gluons, systems that are at least a hundred million times smaller than atoms. That is a very impressive record of achievement. But the paradox is this: that though we can use it, though we know how to do the sums, and though the sums always seem to give us the right answers, we do not understand the theory. We do not know what is going on. That is very odd, and I want to discuss it.

When I say we do not understand what is going on, at one level we know what makes quantum theory different from the mechanics that preceded it. At the level of formalism, it is perfectly clear what is going on. I learned my quantum theory straight from the horse's mouth, from Paul Dirac. He was one of the founding fathers, and he gave a famous lecture course on the principles of quantum mechanics in Cambridge. I would recommend his famous book *The Principles of Quantum Mechanics* (Clarendon Press, 1958). The lectures followed the book closely, and he gave them for about thirty or forty years in Cambridge. Dirac was a clear lecturer but not at all given to rhetoric. Incidentally, it was very impressive that he never in any way stressed his own considerable contributions to quantum theory. He was not given to gestures, except that near the beginning of the course he did do one thing that I remember vividly. He took a piece of chalk, broke it in half, and said, "With a piece of chalk, there is a state where it is here, and there is a state where it is there. And those are just the two possible states. Now if we replace the piece of chalk by an electron, not only is there a state where it is here, and a state where it is there, but there are also states that are formed by superposition, by the adding together of those two basic states." It is the superposition principle — the fact that in quantum theory you can mix together things that in classical physics are simply separate and cannot be mixed — that, at the level of formalism, is the thing that makes the difference between quantum theory and classical mechanics. That is very clear and well understood.

The superposition principle lies behind what Dick Feynman in the third volume of the Feynman Lectures described as *the* essential quantum mechanical phenomenon. Perhaps you remember that double slit experiment. We have a screen with two slits; on one side of it there is some sort of source of quantum entities (let us say it is some sort of electron gun that sprays the apparatus with electrons); and on the other side there is a detecting screen. We all know what happens. Turn the volume down on the gun so it just delivers electrons one at a time, traversing the system. The electrons arrive one by one at the detecting screen. Suppose that the detecting screen, rather unrealistically, is an array of Geiger counters. Then we hear a series of clicks as the electrons arrive. "Click," "click," "click," and so on. That is the particle aspect of electron behavior; the electrons arrive one by one. However, when we collect together the pattern that is formed by all those arrivals, we find, lo and behold, that that pattern takes the form of a typical diffraction pattern. In other words, it is not at all what it would be classically. Classically, we would have just two distributions, one corresponding to the electron going through one slit (which would give you a spike opposite it), and one corresponding electron going through the other slit (which would give you a spike opposite it). But quantum mechanically we do not get that; we get the wave interference pattern, which peaks opposite neither slit. That is the wave aspect of the electron manifesting itself. Now the $64,000 question is, Which slit did the electron go through? Suppose it went through the top slit. If it went through the top slit, it would be irrelevant whether the bottom slit was open or not, and so you would get a peak opposite that slit. If it went through the bottom slit, you would get a peak opposite that slit. You get neither of those, so it neither goes through the top slit nor goes through the bottom slit. That good and wise man Sherlock Holmes said that when you have eliminated the impossible, whatever remains, however improbable, may be the answer to the problem. Therefore we conclude, impeccably, that the indivisible electron went through both slits! Only if we reach that conclusion can we arrive at a diffraction pattern of the type that we actually observe with a peak in the middle. In terms of our picturable everyday world, that is totally paradoxical. But what we mean by that is precisely the superposition principle, that the state of motion of the electron is an adding together of the state in which it went through one slit and the state in which it went through the other slit. In this case, if everything is symmetrical, it is an even-handed superposition. The reason the mathematics of quantum theory is the mathematics of Hilbert spaces is precisely because quantum theory is based on adding things together, upon superposition.

All that is very straightforward if surprising, but it is well understood. The problem comes when we come to the act of measurement. We have an electron in a state that is a mixture of here and there. Suppose now we address to it the experimental question, Where are you? We measure the electron's position.

On each occasion of measurement we get a singly unambiguous answer. We get the answer either "here" or "there." Of course, we usually do not get the same answer on each occasion. That is where the probabilistic aspect comes in. But on each occasion of measurement, we get an actual answer that is not subject to any sort of uncertainty or ambiguity. And the question that we do not know how to answer is, How does it come about, on a particular occasion of experimental inquiry, that we get a particular answer for the position of the electron? In the jargon of the subject, that is sometimes described as the problem of the collapse of the wave packet. The wave packet (the wave function) of the electron is spread out representing assignment of probabilities to a whole range of possible positions. We make a measurement of position, and suddenly all that probability collapses on the single realized position, namely, here. And the question is, How does that come about? How do we get definite measurements in quantum theory? The embarrassing answer is that we do not know. But let me explain some of the problems in trying to sort out that question.

Consider a slightly different form of measurement. To make things simple, I have referred to "here" and "there," but of course electron position can be spread around in a three-dimensional way. Let me now discuss a genuinely two-dimensional possibility. It requires a knowledge of how quantum theory deals with angular momentum. I hope that non-physicist readers will be content to believe what I say. We will consider a spin -½ particle like a proton; we will consider measuring its component in some particular direction. We know then, from quantum theory, that there are only two possible answers; either the spin is up or the spin is down. How do we make such a measurement? We have a beam of protons coming along that is an unpolarized beam that is an evenhanded mixture of spin-up and spin-down. The measurement process is a Stern-Gerlach experiment. An inhomogeneous magnetic field, through its magnetic effects, deflects the protons differently according to the direction of their spin. Suppose that if the spin of the electron is up, it is deviated in direction A, and if the spin is down, it is deviated in direction B. We need some device to determine which way it goes, so we put in a couple of Geiger counters — A and B. Then we see which one clicks, and that will determine a spin measurement for that particular proton.

Now let us think about that process. If the spin is up, then it is deviated in this direction; it then impinges upon counter A, and then I hear counter A click. Or, if the spin is down, then it is deviated in that direction; it then encounters counter B, and then I hear counter B click. In that description, what I have said is, "If, then that, then the next thing." Each possibility is a chain of correlated consequence. If the spin is up, then this happens, then that happens. On the other hand, if the spin is down, then this, then that. And the question is, Where along that chain of correlated consequence does it come about that a particular option is selected on a particular occasion? Every actual measurement is the transmission and amplification of a signal from the microscopic world of the quantum entity into the macroscopic world of the observer. Where does it come about that it is the top branch (A) that is actually activated in this particular measurement rather than the bottom branch (B). From the formalism, I cannot extract that, for from the formalism I just extract this evenhanded correlated consequence account — if one, then that; if the other, then the other. We must try to go beyond that if we are to understand fully what is happening.

Let me distinguish the measurement problem from something we do understand. We do understand very straightforwardly how it comes about that large systems behave, essentially, classically. We understand how quantum mechanics can recover for macroscopic objects the successes of Newtonian mechanics, but that is *not* the solution of the measurement problem. That understanding simply tells us that the successive links along one of those chains of correlated consequence get tighter and tighter as we go from the small to the large. But it does not tell us what selects this chain of correlated consequence from that chain of correlated consequence — that selection effect which is the essence of the measurement problem. It is important to get that distinction clear in our minds. Otherwise, we will not see what the problem is.

Returning to the real problem, what have been the various suggestions that have been made? My list will probably not be exhaustive, but I will offer some suggested explanations. This problem came up in the early days of quantum theory. The great pioneers of the subject had to face it. The story of quantum theory in the middle 1920s is the story of a grand old man, papa Bohr, a sort of philosopher king sitting in his court in Copenhagen with all the bright young people — Heisenberg, Schroedinger, Dirac, and others — coming to bring their thoughts and tributes to the philosopher king. Papa Bohr said yes or no, and that was that. This is something of a caricature, but it contains an element of the history of the early days of modern quantum theory. Bohr was the philosopher king, so the resolution of the measurement problem was really left to him. He pronounced what is commonly called the Copenhagen interpretation. In that interpretation he essentially said that it is the intervention of classical measuring apparatus that brings about a particular result on a particular occasion. It is the classical measuring apparatus that does the trick. Aha! you might say, but what is classical measuring apparatus? Bohr said effectively that there are two sorts of stuff in the world. There are quantum entities, and there is classical measuring apparatus. It is the juxtaposition of the two, the clamping of the two together, that produces a particular result on a particular occasion. So Bohr had what a philosopher would have called a "dualist" view of the physical world. To him there were two different sorts of stuff — quantum entities and measuring apparatus. In those terms, there is a sort of shallow consistency about that interpretation. There are difficulties about where you draw the line between the two. Bohr insisted that you had to clamp the two together in what he called a phenomenon — an act of measurement — and then you could draw the dividing line in slightly different places and it would not matter. But you had these two sorts of stuff, and you needed both to get a result. Amazingly enough, people were content with that for a very long time. I think that was partly because intellectual exhaustion set in after the terrific discoveries of quantum theory. Yet when we stop to think about it, we can see that this cannot possibly be an adequate solution to the problem, because the physical world does not consist of two sorts of stuff. It consists of only one sort of stuff. Moreover, what is that classical measuring apparatus made of? It is made of electrons and protons and neutrons — in other words, of quantum entities. There are not two sorts of stuff.

So the question remains, How does it come about that things that are made out of constituents that belong to that probabilistic, elusive, indeterminate quantum world become classical measuring apparatus, with this amazing property of determining the results of a quantum measurement? That is the problem that Bohr refused to address. So it was a solution, if you like, by neglect, by oversimplification. I think that there would not be too many people today who would consider that a satisfactory resolution of the problem. However, you might think, even if he did not get it right, at least he was looking in the right direction. And the right direction might mean something like this: one of the things that is connected with classical measurement apparatus is certainly that it is large. And maybe what is going on is the transition from small to large so that, somewhere along that chain, when things become sufficiently big, they acquire, in an emergent way, this new property of being determinators rather than being undetermined objects. There is a kind of neo-Copenhagen interpretation that says, putting it crudely, that making things large does the trick for you. My personal inclination is to think that that is the right direction in which to look. But it is no more than an expression of pious hope at this stage, and it will not become more than that until we understand or are able to give an account of how increasing largeness brings about this new property of determination, of acting as classical measuring apparatus. There are a few straws in the wind that may be suggestive.

For instance, there is another emergence that we are familiar with (though again we do not totally understand it) that happens when we go from the small to the large. It is connected with the question of irreversibility. We know that the laws of physics, on the microscopic scale, are reversible. There is no intrinsic direction of time, no intrinsic distinction between past and future. If I could make a film — which of course Heisenberg will not let me do — of two protons interacting with each other, I would not be able to tell whether the film was being run forward or backward. It would make equal physical sense either way. So microscopic processes are reversible, but macroscopic processes are not. If I show a film of a bouncing ball in which the bounces get higher and higher, you know I am running the system backward. So there is an emergent irreversibility that we think is somehow connected with thermodynamic effects, with increasing entropy.

We do not understand the direction of the arrow of time very well; but at least the solution to the two problems — the problem of irreversibility and the problem of measurement — might very well be linked together, because one of the things that measurement involves is the irreversible registration of a result. Measurement is a time-asymmetric process. Before the measurement you are ignorant; after the measurement you know. So it also has an intrinsic direction of time, a distinction between past and future, built into it. I have a feeling that the solution to the measurement problem may very well lie along these lines. But that has to be worked out; and until that has been done this idea is no more than waving one's arms in a mildly hopeful direction that is not quite enough to produce the solution to the problem.

Because of the restless ingenuity of theoretical physicists, a number of other possible solutions to the problem have been proposed. Let me describe some. The second group of solutions could be summarized under the heading of "No Problem." They essentially say that you were mistaken in thinking that there is a difficulty. There is an unsophisticated form of that answer, and there is a much more sophisticated form of the answer. The unsophisticated form is to deny that quantum mechanics is concerned with individual events anyway. Things are always made more dignified if given a name, and so the unsophisticated form is called the ensemble interpretation. It says that quantum mechanics does not pretend to speak about individual events; it is agnostic about individual events. It simply speaks about what will happen in a great collection of events, an ensemble of measurements. That is the ensemble interpretation. On that interpretation there is no problem, but there is no problem by definition. We have committed intellectual suicide in setting the problem aside. I cannot for a moment accept that as a valid strategy. The purpose of physics is to investigate the processes of the physical world in as much detail and with as much coherence as we possibly can. To throw in the sponge by simply saying we cannot speak about individual events does not seem to me a fitting strategy for a physicist. So I just reject the ensemble interpretation as being inadequate physics.

A much more interesting solution, which in the end says there is no problem, is the alternative interpretation of quantum mechanics that was invented by David Bohm. There has always been a feeling that maybe quantum theory is not so strange, not so different, after all. Maybe quantum mechanical entities are unproblematic and behave just like ordinary Newtonian particles, and the fuzziness that we attribute to them is due simply to ignorance, rather than being an intrinsic property they possess. In other words, perhaps quantum mechanics is like statistical physics in that we just see certain aspects of what is going on and average over the unknown aspects of the situation. In the trade, that idea is called "hidden variables," referring to aspects that are not available to us in our investigation. For example, if you have a collection of radioactive atoms, half of which are going to decay in the next hour, maybe each of them has some little clock that tells it precisely when to decay. Those clocks are so set that half of them will go off in the course of the hour. Unfortunately, we are unable to read those clocks, so it looks to us as if it is purely a probabilistic event. But John von Neumann, who after all, was quite a good mathematician, was thought to have shown that the probabilities involved in quantum theory took a certain form that did not permit you to have a hidden variable interpretation. It was therefore something of a surprise in the 1950s when David Bohm came along and produced a theory that had precisely that property. People went back and had a look at von Neumann's argument, and they found that he had made a tiny little technical assumption that looked quite harmless, but in fact was very harmful. He was assuming the answer that he wanted, and that assumption was something that was not true in quantum mechanical systems. So then, be forewarned against believing even the greatest of men all the time!

Bohm's idea was very clever, but there is a problem for a realistic theory of this kind. Let us go back to that double slit experiment. If the electron is a particle like any other particle, then of course it must go through just one of the slits. So, how do I get around the argument I presented that it had to go through both? What I said was that it would have to make a difference to this particle if it went through one slit whether the other slit was open or not. Bohm found a way of putting in that difference and thereby producing exactly the same experimental consequences as in conventional quantum theory. The way he did it was immensely clever. He did it by divorcing wave and particle. In conventional quantum theory, wave and particle are just complementary aspects of the one entity; an electron is sometimes a wave, sometimes a particle. But in Bohm's theory, there are particles, which I have already said are as uncontroversially particles as any Newtonian could possibly want, but there is also a hidden wave that is different. That wave encapsulates information about the whole environment. We do not see it directly; it is not directly physically observable. But because it is a wave and so spread out, and because also it possesses certain instantaneous properties, it knows about the whole environment. Thus the wave knows whether the other slit is open or not, and if I close it, the wave will change instantaneously. Furthermore, the wave is what is called a pilot wave. That is to say, it does have a hidden influence, which is to guide the direction of the electron. It represents an extra influence acting upon the electron over and above all the things that classical physics knew about. So, it turns out that if I shut the other slit, the wave knows about it, and it makes the electron instantaneously move in a different way. One could set that theory up in such a way that when the slit was closed the wave made the electron peak one way, and when the slit was open it made the electron move in another, just like ordinary quantum theory. It was a very clever and very surprising thing to be able to do.

Thus we actually face in quantum theory two different theories, exactly equivalent in terms of their empirical consequences, but with an *entirely different* interpretation. This is the only example I can think of in fundamental physics in which that actually happens, but here it does. Yet it turns out that nearly everybody believes conventional quantum theory, and not many people, except for Bohm and his immediate friends, believe his theory. Why is that? Bohm's theory is very clever, but there is a feeling that it is too clever by half. There is an air of contrivance about the theory. One might think, here is a theory that should win the day because it is simple; it is picturable. But people do not like it because they feel very suspicious about this hidden wave. It multiplies entities. The wave has a little bit of a feel to it of the luminiferous ether of the nineteenth century, and that, of course, is a very pejorative thing to say. There is also an air of contrivance about the way the theory is set up. The wave has to satisfy some sort of wave equation. What wave equation does it satisfy? You will not be surprised to learn that it satisfies the Schroedinger equation. Why does it satisfy the Schroedinger equation? Because we will not get the right answers unless it does. Would Bohm have thought of that if he had not already known about the Schroedinger equation? I cannot answer that question, but there is an air of contrivance about this interpretation that has made it very unpersuasive.

There is something interesting here. Sometimes people say that really what matters in science is empirical adequacy. That is not true. Empirical adequacy is necessary but is not sufficient for a convincing and successful scientific theory. There must be something fitting, economic, and elegant about the theory. And many of us feel, despite the extraordinary ingenuity of Bohm's ideas, that he does not quite score on that basis.

Let us go on and think about some other possibilities. Recall the chain of consequence. If the spin is up in that direction, then it goes this way, then it hits the Geiger counter, then I hear the Geiger counter click. At the end of every chain of known experimental observation there is the intervention of the consciousness of an observer, because otherwise we would not know what the answer was. There are people who have suggested that *that* is the point along the chain at which the matter gets settled. At first sight there is a certain sort of specious attractiveness about that. It is hard to say when things get large enough to make the difference, but the intervention of consciousness — that mysterious interface between mind and matter — does seem to bring something qualitatively new into the correlated chain of consequence. We know that the physical world acts upon the mind because that is how we know about the physical world around us. Perhaps the mind acts back upon the physical world, and perhaps the way that it does this is by determining the results of quantum observations. So my third possibility is that consciousness, which is always there at the end of the chain, is the feature that brings it about. This theory has been espoused by some quite distinguished people, most notably by Eugene Wigner, who won a Nobel Prize for physics and so is entitled to a certain amount of respectful attention. Once again, however, I am not persuaded that *that* can be the answer to the problem.

There are two difficulties about this line of attack. The first is, Which sort of consciousness does the trick? How fully conscious do things have to be in order to produce a resolution of a quantum measurement? We all know the sad tale of

Schroedinger's cat. That unfortunate animal is encased within a box in which there is a radioactive source that has a 50/50 chance of decaying in the next hour. If it decays, the radiation will trigger the breaking of a vial of poison gas and the cat will be killed. If it does not decay, the cat will live. If I approach that closed box at the end of the hour and I apply conventional quantum theory to it from the outside, that theory tells me that the cat is in an evenhanded superposition of alive and dead. It is only when I open the box that I will find a cooling corpse or a frisking feline. But that cannot be right, can it? The cat must know whether it is dead or not, without my having to intervene. So if consciousness does it, the consciousness of the cat presumably must be sufficient to achieve the end. Where do you stop? Will a worm do it? Are worms conscious? I do not know. So that is one problem — to know where to draw the line.

The second problem is that there is something very strange about this whole interpretation. Most of the time and in most places in cosmic history, consciousness has not been present. Does that mean that for most of cosmic history, and in most places in the present universe, quantum events have not had a determined outcome? Well, maybe, but it takes a bit of swallowing. Let us do a sort of terrestrial version of that. Suppose I set up, as one could easily do, a computerized measuring scheme for a quantum experiment, and I arrange for the computer to print out the result of the experiment and store it away unseen in a drawer. I approach the drawer six months later and open it; I am the first person to look at that piece of paper. If it is consciousness that brings about the definite result, until the moment six months later when I open that drawer, there was not definite imprint upon the paper. That is possible, but again it takes a bit of swallowing. So I think that consciousness does not provide the solution to this particular problem.

So we move on. The consciousness solution is slightly bizarre, but nowhere near as bizarre as the next solution, which is that *everything* happens. This is the celebrated (or notorious, according to taste) "many worlds" interpretation of quantum

theory invented by Hugh Everett. It says that the formalism
is your guide — take it seriously. The formalism is based upon
superposition, and it is perfectly evenhanded between all the
different possibilities. It is a superposition of up and a superposition of down, a superposition of counter A clicking and a
superposition of counter B clicking, and so forth. "Okay," says
Dr. Everett, "take that seriously; everything that might happen
does happen." Schroedinger's cat is alive; Schroedinger's cat is
dead. There is a problem with that, obviously, because why
does the Schroedinger cat that lived have the impression that
it lived? Perhaps the one that died did not have that impression
that it died, but at least *we* have the impression that it died. So
if everything happens, there must also be some sort of dividing
up of the world, of the universe, into parallel, disjoint worlds
in which all different mutually exclusive possibilities are actually realized. In other words, at the end of the Schroedinger's
cat experiment, there is a universe split in two — one continuing universe in which Schroedinger's cat lives and another
continuing universe in which Schroedinger's cat dies. And the
fact that those two universes are disjoint saves the Schroedinger
cat that lives from schizophrenic difficulties about the one that
died. That is the proposal. It is a proposal of absolutely stag-
gering prodigality because quantum mechanical measurements
are being made all the time; therefore, all the time the world is
dividing. Our belief in a single continuous biography is some
sort of curious and unexplained trick of the way human per-
ception works. Poor old William of Ockam must be turning
in his grave at the thought of this theory. I am totally unper-
suaded by the "many worlds" quantum theory, and so are most
physicists, except for one recognizable group. They are those
who have the ambition to apply quantum theory to the whole
universe, the quantum cosmologists. If you are going to apply
quantum theory to the whole universe, you do not have anything left to you. You have no external observer; you have no
large piece of measuring apparatus, nothing left over to refer
to. So if you are going to apply quantum theory to the whole

universe, you are driven to a "many worlds" interpretation for doing it.

I offer two comments on that. First, it is not obvious to me that it is a feasible and sensible program to apply quantum mechanics to the whole universe. The universe is a different sort of entity from any subsystem contained within it; and because we do not actually understand how quantum theory relates to the everyday world, it seems to me slightly overambitious to leapfrog that and apply it to the whole universe. Second, there seems to me an astonishing lack of candor, particularly in the semipopular literature about quantum cosmology, in recognizing that it implies many conflicting, yet in some sense realized, histories for the universe. So, although this is an interpretation that has greatly appealed to the sort of "gee whiz" section of scientific journalists, frankly it does not appeal to me at all.

We have almost come to the end of the tale. There is an additional possibility, and this is, in my mind, of equal likelihood with some version of the neo-Copenhagen interpretation. What we see here is the possibility that there is new physics involved in the quantum measurement process. Once you start moving into that area, there are a variety of possibilities that could be canvassed. I will briefly mention a few.

One is the proposal of three people — Girardi, Rimini, and Weber (GRW). This proposal says that quantum measurement involves collapses and jumps. Perhaps the world is just like that. Perhaps these discontinuities take place all the time, but the way they take place is correlated with the number of particles present in the participating system. This is a very clever proposal. Girardi, Rimini, and Weber propose a sort of jumpy mechanism, a discontinuous mechanism whose effect is proportional to "N," the number of particles present. In other words, when "N equals 1," and when a quantum entity is on its own, then these things happen extraordinarily rarely, perhaps every hundred million years, so we do not notice them for a single entity. But when you get a rather large number of entities to the order of "10^{23}," or some macroscopic number like that, then these jumps happen essentially instantaneously. It is a clever proposal to produce a new physics that will make large systems have this effect simply because large systems induce jumps and they induce the right sort of jumps. The merit is that, if there really is new physics there, you could try to look for it. You could look for systems with "N" somewhere in between "1" and "10^{23}" and determine whether you saw jumps taking place, but over a modest period. This proposal has not, as far as I am aware, gained a very large number of adherents. Again, it is clever but contrived. That is the trouble with all these theories.

Another example is a theory produced by Roger Penrose. Perhaps you have read *The Emperor's New Mind,* which is an exciting if somewhat self-indulgent book written by an old friend of mine. Roger, of course, is a very clever chap, and he has had many interests. One of his interests is the relationship between quantum mechanics and gravity, which is an unsolved problem. Most people think that that will be solved by tinkering with gravity so that you replace general relativity by superstrings, for example. But Penrose thinks it will be solved by tinkering with quantum theory. He suggests that when you do that, the measurement effect becomes a sort of quantum gravity effect. That is an amazing thought! I think it would be fair to say that it is a thought that has not been worked out in every detail in the book. However, one of its consequences would involve the size a system has to be to produce a definite result. It will be Planck mass, which is "10^{-5} grams," which is enormously large in atomic terms. Here again is another possibility for new physics. But I must say, I raise a slightly skeptical eyebrow.

There are, no doubt, some other theories that could be considered. I think, broadly speaking, I have given a survey of the options that are being tried to solve this extremely central problem for the understanding of quantum theory. And my feeling is that in our present state of knowledge none of these solutions is wholly acceptable. We really do not know what the answer is. so, in a sense, I have a tale without an ending. However, I must finish, so, because I am a clergyman, I will draw a moral from this tale. The moral, I think, is that explanation and understanding are two different things. We can use quantum theory to explain very successfully a great many things about the world in which we live, from superconductivity to subatomic particle physics. But we do not *understand* quantum theory. Explanation and understanding are two different things. I think the final moral I would like to draw from this is that however seriously we take science, we should not put it on a pedestal and think (a) that it is different from other forms of human inquiry and (b) that it knows all the answers, because it is perfectly obvious that it does not. Moreover, in a remarkable way, it can live without knowing all the answers. We should not be complacent about not understanding the measurement problem in quantum theory, but equally, we can do quite a lot of interesting things without having solved that particular problem. That again is a lesson that has a wider application in physics alone.

- Three -

TAKING SCIENCE
SERIOUSLY

I HAVE SPENT most of my working life as a theoretical physicist. All my life I have been a member of the worshiping
and believing community of the church, and for the last ten
years I have been an Anglican priest. Consequently, I am someone who wants to take both science and theology seriously, and
in this and the next chapter I hope to explore a little of what
that might imply. This chapter will be concerned with science,
and in the following chapter you will see that theology offers
both parallels and explanatory connections with what we will
be thinking about in this chapter. There are eight assertions I
want to make about science.

1. *Science is concerned with the rational exploration of what is
the case.* In other words, science is the search for an understanding of the nature and pattern of the physical world. That may
seem an obvious thing to say; most scientists would be astonished to learn that there was any other way of thinking about
their subject. After all, what else would make worthwhile all
the weary labor and frustration involved in scientific research if
it were not the thought that in the end we would learn something new about the way the world is? Yet many philosophers
in the twentieth century have suggested that this is not what

34

science is about at all. They see difficulties in the claim that science tells it like it is. They point out that its procedures are not as straightforward as people think.

A popular view of how science works is that someone makes a prediction on the basis of a theory. Then an experiment is done to see if the prediction works, and if it does, the theory is verified. But this simple picture of the unambiguous confrontation of theory and experiment does not hold up to careful consideration. The trouble is that theory and experiment are intertwined in subtle ways that are hard to disentangle. You might show me some marks on a photographic plate, and we would no doubt agree on the pattern they formed. But that pattern by itself is of no real interest. It only becomes so when it is *theoretically* interpreted as indicating the decay of an Ω particle. All significant scientific facts are theory laden. In a famous phrase, we can look at the physical world only by wearing "spectacles behind the eyes"; we view it from an adopted perspective through which we interpret and select out from the flux of events what is truly significant. If that is the case, perhaps the results of science are just "an agreement to see it that way," the way unconsciously chosen by the invisible college of scientists under the pressures of communal expectation. Philosophers who take this view claim that the physicist's picture of the world is the result of social construction rather than true discovery. The success of science is only a purely instrumental success, the attainment of manners of speaking that are effective in getting things done but not in describing things as they actually are. Talk of electrons is a way of constructing devices like the electron microscope, not a discovery of what matter is actually made of. So the story goes.

I am quite sure that this is wrong. I nail my colors to the realist mast and assert that science is the rational exploration of what is the case.[1] For the present, two considerations must suffice in defense of this position.

The first is to ask what could make these manners of speaking so effective if it were not that they describe the way things are. The idea of electrons enables us not only to make electron microscopes but also to do many other things, such as work with superconducting devices and understand much of chemistry. The only rational explanation of this widespread success is that there actually are electrons that behave in the ways that physics describes. Any other account would make sustained instrumental success a mysterious miracle.

Second, the whole feel of doing science is one of discovery and not construction. Time and again the physical world resists our expectation, and we have to struggle very hard to understand it. Far from our molding our experiences into pleasing shapes of our own choosing, we are continually challenged and surprised by what we encounter.

Yet the criticisms of the philosophers do teach us some useful things. Science is not as straightforward an activity as we might have supposed without their analysis. We do wear "spectacles behind the eyes." We can approach the physical world only from a previously chosen point of view. In another famous phrase, selected this time from theology, even in science we have to "believe in order to understand." Of course, that initial belief must be open to correction in the light of subsequent investigation. That is what makes science a *rational* activity. It is also, as Michael Polanyi argued so cogently, a *personal* activity.[2] By that I mean that it involves acts of judgment of a kind that cannot be delegated to computers but that must be made by people who have acquired tacit skills in the course of an apprenticeship to a living, intellectual tradition. For example, in any experiment one must eliminate what is called background, the unwanted spurious events arising from causes other than the phenomena we are trying to investigate. The assessment that this has been done successfully rests on experience and intuition, and it can never be reduced to the following of a set of rules.

We are right to take science seriously, but not because it is wholly different in character from all other forms of rational inquiry. All such quests for truth involve an inescapable degree of intellectual daring, a necessary commitment to a corrigible point of view that is the only basis for attaining deeper understanding. Once we have recognized that, the very success of science in its own rational endeavor will encourage us to take with equal seriousness other attempts to explore different aspects of the many-layered reality of our experience.

2. *The physical world is marvelously rationally transparent.* We are so used to understanding the physical world that most of the time we take this for granted. It makes science possible, but surely it is a very significant aspect of the way things are. In particular, let us pause to recognize, in Eugene Wigner's pregnant phrase, the "unreasonable effectiveness of mathematics." It is our continual experience that the mathematical expressions of the theories that describe the universe are endowed with the unmistakable character of mathematical beauty. Why should this be so? After all, mathematics arises from the free explorations of the human mind, but some of its most elegant and harmonious patterns are found actually to occur in the world around us. So characteristic is this of the discoveries of physics that Paul Dirac once said that it was more important in framing a theory to have beauty in one's equations than to have them fit experiment! Of course, he did not mean that empirical success was unimportant, but that its apparent failure might be due to bad calculations or even erroneous experiments. But to have ugly equations would be an irredeemable disaster. They could not be right.

Mathematics proves to be the key to unlock the secrets of the universe. Why should this be so? Why do the reason within (mathematics) and the reason without (physics) fit together so perfectly? Einstein once said that the only incomprehensible thing about the universe is that it is comprehensible.

Of course, at the everyday level, evolutionary biology provides an explanation. If our ordinary thoughts did not fit our ordinary experience, we would not have survived in the struggle for existence. But the unreasonable effectiveness of mathematics is a much more profound fact than anything that such banal considerations could explain. It applies to the counterintuitive quantum world, in its probabilistic elusiveness, so very different from the world of everyday experience. That world is unpicturable for us in its strangeness, but it is not unintelligible to us, though its understanding demands the use of very abstract and sophisticated mathematics. I cannot believe that our power to conceive of such mathematics is just a spin-off from our ancestors, who have had to dodge the attacks of saber-toothed tigers.

Science itself cannot explain the rational transparency of the physical world (which makes its enterprise possible) nor the rational beauty of that world (whose discovery makes science worthwhile). It is part of the founding faith of science that this should be so. Yet it does not seem sufficient just to say, "That's the way it is, and a bit of good luck for you chaps who happen to be good at math!" In the intelligibility of the physical world we encounter an insight derived from science and calling for an explanation, even though that explanation is beyond science's power to offer. One could call the universe's intelligibility a signal of transcendence, an intimation that there is more to understand than has met the scientific eye.

3. *The fruitful history of the universe depends upon fine-tuning in its physical laws and circumstance.* This is the insight of the celebrated anthropic principle.[3]

Our universe started very simply, fifteen billion years ago. It was then just a uniform expanding ball of energy. Today it is richly varied, containing within it such interesting and complicated consequences as you and me. The tale of cosmic evolution is one of an astonishing fruitfulness. At least in outline, we have attained a good deal of scientific understanding of the processes by which that fertile history came about. We can also play intellectual games (with serious intent) and consider how things might have gone if the universe had been somewhat different. For instance, suppose the force of gravity had been a bit stronger than it is, or electromagnetism a bit weaker. I imagine that one would have expected that such changes would modify things, but not in a drastic way. It has been surprising, therefore, to realize that in fact quite small changes in any of these basic physical laws would have rendered cosmic history boring and sterile. A fruitful world — a world capable of evolving *anthrōpoi* — is a very special universe. Its finely tuned laws make it a cosmos in a trillion.

Many considerations point to that surprising conclusion. Let me sketch just two of them. A fruitful universe must have the right sort of stars in it. They have two indispensable roles to play. One is as providers of energy for life. There must be stars capable of burning steadily for billions of years, just as our sun has been doing. The second role is to provide the chemical elements that are the raw materials for life. Because the very early universe is very simple, it can make only the two simplest elements, hydrogen and helium. They do not provide the possibility for a rich enough chemistry to enable life to develop. For that, one needs heavier elements like carbon and oxygen. These can be made only in the nuclear furnaces of stars. Every atom of carbon in our bodies was once inside a star; we are all made from the ashes of dead stars. And if the elements thus made are actually to be available for the evolution of life, they must be accessible by the supernova explosion of some of these stars as they reach the end of their nuclear lives. It turns out that these stellar requirements place very tight limitations on all the intrinsic forces of nature if they are to prove capable of fulfillment.

The second consideration is the size of the universe. Our cosmos contains at least 10^{22} stars. It is unimaginably vast, and sometimes we feel daunted at the thought of such immensity. We should not, for if all those trillions of stars were not there, we would not be here to be upset by the thought of them. Only a universe as big as ours could have lasted the fifteen billion years that are needed to make men and women. It is a process that cannot be hurried.

The anthropic principle represents a kind of anti-Copernican revolution in our cosmological thinking. We do not live at the center of the universe, but neither do we live in just "any old world." Instead, we live in a universe whose constitution is precisely adjusted to the narrow limits that alone would make it capable of being our home. Once more we encounter what one might consider to be a signal of transcendence. Science does not explain its own laws; they are the given foundation of its endeavor. Yet those laws do not seem, in their anthropic fine-tuning, to be without the demand for some further explanation. It is scarcely enough to say, "We're here because we're here, and that's that." Is there something happening in what is going on in the physical universe that raises cosmic process beyond the level of mere brute occurrence?

4. *The physical world is endowed with true becoming.* In the eighteenth and nineteenth centuries, people thought of the universe as if it were a gigantic piece of cosmic clockwork. The twentieth century has seen the death of such a merely mechanical account. Whatever the universe is, it is something more subtle and more supple than that. In part, this realization stems from the cloudy unpredictability of quantum mechanics, lurking at the subatomic roots of the world. But more significantly still, we have recently come to realize that even the physics of the everyday is not as mechanical as we once thought it to be. This insight is given the somewhat inapt name of the dynamical theory of chaos.[4] It turns out that even in a Newtonian universe, most systems of any degree of complexity are so exquisitely sensitive to the finest detail of their circumstance that their behavior is radically unpredictable. You will not be surprised that this first came to light from studies of models of the weather! It is sometimes called the butterfly effect, which asserts that the earth's weather systems are so sensitive that a butterfly stirring the air with its wings in China today will have consequences for the storms over Canada within a few weeks. Because we cannot possibly know about all those Chinese butterflies, we cannot reliably predict what will happen in the future.

This profound unpredictability is very surprising, but one might argue that it is just an expression of our ignorance. I want to say more than that. We physicists are realists. On our T-shirts we have written the rousing slogan "Epistemology Models Ontology"; what we can know is a guide to what is actually the case. On that understanding, our ignorance of the future is to be interpreted as the sign that that future is, in fact, open. Hence my claim that we live in a world of true becoming.

Of course, we did not need the insights of the dynamical theory of chaos to tell us that. Our basic human experiences of choice and action make that clear enough. But it is a gain for *physics* if it can begin to describe a world of which we can, with consistency, consider ourselves as being inhabitants. I have suggested that the extra causal principles that bring about an actual future within the open possibilities of a world of becoming have the character of "active information" and represent a kind of top-down causality operating within wholes, which complements the bottom-up energetic causality of parts (which is what physics describes).[5] We begin to get the faintest glimmer of how mind and matter might relate in our experience of human agency. In chapter 4 I will explore how this idea might also provide a way of thinking about divine providential action in a manner that is fully consistent with all that we know scientifically about physical process.

5. *The physical world is often surprising.* If the study of science teaches one anything, it is not to take everyday thought as the measure of all that is. In fact, the continually surprising character of the physical world is one of those features that rewards the scientific investigator. One never knows what unexpected aspect is next to be revealed.

The degree to which commonsense notions prove in need of revision is often very considerable, extending in the case of quantum theory even to logic itself. If I say to you that Bill is at home and that he is either drunk or sober, you will deduce that either you will find Bill at home drunk or you will find him at home sober. The learned would say that you have applied the distributive law of logic to reach this apparently harmless conclusion. Yet if we replace Bill by an electron, or any other quantum entity, the same line of argument no longer applies. That is because classical logic, as codified by Aristotle, depends upon the law of the excluded middle; it has no middle term between (A) or (not A). That sharp either/or is removed by quantum theory, which permits the probabilistic adding together of possibilities that common sense would declare unmixable. An electron can be in a state that is a mixture of (here) and (not here), which yields a possibility undreamed of by Aristotle: (sometimes here). In consequence, a new kind of logic, quantum logic, had to be invented by Birkhoff and von Neumann to deal with this situation.

One of the general consequences of the discovery of quantum theory has been to enlarge our imagination of what is possible. In 1900 it would have seemed obvious that entities could be waves (spread out and flapping up and down) or little particles (small bullets) but not both. We all know that light and all other quantum entities nevertheless sometimes behave in a wavelike way and sometimes in a particlelike way. It is less widely recognized that in 1927 Paul Dirac invented a formalism (quantum field theory) that perfectly reconciles these behaviors without a taint of paradox. Quantum theory delivers us from an undue tyranny of common sense.

6. *The investigation of the pattern and structure of the physical world is exciting.* Like every worthwhile activity, science has its weary routine and the frustrations that come from lines of inquiry that eventually prove fruitless. At the end of the day, the wastepaper basket of a theoretical physicist is likely to contain a lot of crumpled pieces of paper. Why then do we do it? The payoff for all that labor is the sense of wonder at the beautiful order revealed to our investigation. There is something deeply intellectually satisfying in the patterns thus revealed. Einstein often spoke of the pleasure he felt in the harmony of natural law. There is a profound character to the structure revealed, which often greatly exceeds our puny prior expectations.

Among the most exciting discoveries in physics have been those unifying insights that reveal that apparently disparate phenomena and effects are in fact the varied manifestations of a single reality. In the nineteenth century, the experimental discoveries of Oersted and Faraday and the theoretical genius of Clerk Maxwell succeeded in unifying electric and magnetic phenomena in the single subject of electromagnetism. In our own century, Steven Weinberg and Abdus Salam (who was my Ph.D. supervisor) showed that, despite striking differences in their properties, electromagnetism and the weak nuclear force (responsible for radioactive decays) are, in fact, the single fruit of a yet more profound synthesis. At present, the search is on for even more general Grand Unified Theories (or GUTs) that will draw the other forces of nature (the strong nuclear force and gravity) into a single account. There are considerable difficulties yet to be surmounted in this ambitious program, but most of us hope and expect that one day it will find its fulfillment.

There is a grandeur in the pattern and structure of the physical world that is profoundly exciting to discover and deeply satisfying to contemplate. The word *wonder* is one that scientists habitually use to describe their experiences and to justify the great endeavor in which they are engaged.

7. *Yet science is problematic.* In the public mind, science is *the* rational activity. I have already explained why I do not think that it is wholly different in kind from other forms of rational inquiry. Its great success stems from its self-limitation to certain types of question (essentially, asking the question, "How? addressed to certain aspects of experience that, because of their objective character, are open to the manipulation and interrogation by means of the experimental method).

Even within these narrow confines, however, science does not succeed at any time in achieving a completely resolved and satisfactory rationality. It proves itself capable of living with unsolved problems — not, of course, with complacency about that situation, but with a realistic acknowledgment of a necessary degree of provisionality about its current understanding. Two examples drawn from twentieth-century science make the point.

Quantum mechanics has been outstandingly empirically successful since its articulation in its modern form in the mid-1920s. Originally conceived of in order to deal with problems in atomic physics, it has proved equally able to cope with the dynamics of quarks and gluons, constituent entities that are a hundred million times smaller than atoms. Yet, although we can use quantum theory to such great effect, we still do not understand it properly. The cause of our perplexity is the measurement problem.[6] How does it come about that the fitful and elusive quantum world yields an unambiguous (if not always identical) answer on each occasion of observational inquiry? The wave function for an electron assigns it a probability for being "here" and a probability for being "there," but when we actually investigate where it is, each time we will receive a definite answer, sometimes "here," sometimes "there," but never both. How does this come about? It is rather humiliating for a physicist to have to say that there is no universally agreed and satisfactory answer to that entirely reasonable question. In chapter 2 I have tried to go into the various rival responses and to discuss the perplexities that bedevil each of them. I do not believe the matter will remain unresolved forever, but it is certainly currently the case that, though quantum theory provides us with many explanations of phenomena, we still have not attained a wholly satisfactory understanding of what it implies about the nature of physical reality.

My second example also involves quantum theory, but in this case it is its relationship to general relativity that I want to discuss. The latter is the modern theory of gravity, but the application of quantum mechanics to it has proved a problem of intractable difficulty. There are hopeful directions in which to look for a resolution of this problem, with the theory of superstrings being the presently favored candidate for its solution, but physics has lived for more than sixty years with two of its fundamental theories imperfectly reconciled with each other.

8. *Science has things to say to theology.* It is impossible to read out a general metaphysical point of view (such as would

be a theological account of what is the case) from the consideration of physics alone. Such a comprehensive understanding must draw upon insights and experience going far beyond the self-limited realm of science itself. Physics does not determine metaphysics, but it certainly constrains it. It is not possible to erect an arbitrary metaphysical edifice upon a given basis of physical understanding. The proper relationship between science and theology is one of consonance; the discoveries of physics will impose constraints upon the tone and character of theological discourse.

We now know that the universe has had a history. Far from the world as we experience it having come into being almost instantaneously and "ready made," it was once very different from the way it is today. Its many-billion-year history of evolving fruitfulness will discourage any thought of a Creator who works by magic. The Creator is not a God in a hurry; rather God is patient and subtle in relation to a world that its Creator has allowed largely to "make itself." The theologian may well reflect that there is unlikely to be any other way in which love would choose to work.[7]

The physical world as science discerns it is one in which order and disorder interlace and fertilize each other. The creative interplay of chance (happenstance — the occurrences that are the seeds of novelty) and necessity (lawful regularity that sifts and preserves the novelties thrown up by happenstance) lies at the root of all the fruitful history of the universe. The theologian must be prepared to reckon with this role of chance.

Physical process is not merely mechanical, but it has an inherent openness that makes this a world of true becoming. The theologian should not only be glad for the hospitality this seems to offer to notions of human and divine agency. He or she should also consider the possibility that in this world of true becoming, it may well be that even God does not yet know the unformed future. This would not be an imperfection in the divine nature, for the future is not yet there to be known.

The cosmologist, peering into the future as well as the past, sees that the universe will eventually end badly — either in the bang of cosmic collapse or in the whimper of cosmic decay. The theologian must be prepared to take on board the scientific certainty that humanity will prove to be only a transient episode in the history of the universe.

There are many ways in which science speaks to theology in a manner to which that subject must be prepared to pay attention. I certainly want to take science seriously, but I want to take the unity of knowledge and the rich diversity of reality even more seriously. It is my firm belief that both science and theology are aspects of a rational inquiry into the way the world is. To deny that and to confine oneself to science alone would be to embrace the impoverished fallacy of scientism.

I have tried to draw attention in this chapter to certain aspects of science that seem to be relevant to the wider quest for knowledge and understanding. In chapter 4 I will try to explore the cousinly relationship between science and theology by paying attention to what it means to take theology seriously. I will suggest that there is a significant degree of parallelism with some of the concerns that have occupied us in this chapter.

– Four –

TAKING THEOLOGY
SERIOUSLY

WHEN I TURNED my collar round and became a clergyman after nearly thirty years of work in science, my
life changed in various ways, but it still continued to be concerned with the search for truth. In that respect, all that altered
was that the truth with which I was then professionally involved was of a more profound and comprehensive kind than in
my scientific days. It is a common contention among scientists
turned theologian that their former and their latter disciplines
are really intellectual cousins under the skin.[1] There are eight
assertions I want to make about theology. You will perceive
that they parallel the eight assertions I made about science in
chapter 3.

1. *Theology is concerned with the rational exploration of what
is the case.* Many people have a picture of theologians as being
concerned with irrational assertion, putting a stop to critical
inquiry by evoking the unchallengeable concept of revelation.
In England, politicians use the adjective *theological* in a pejorative sense, denoting mysterious and ill-founded claims. I want
to say as strongly as I can that such an understanding of the
theological enterprise is a travesty of it.

Religious belief is not a question of shutting one's eyes, gritting one's teeth, and believing the impossible. Faith involves an act of commitment, but that commitment is *motivated;* it is a leap into the light and not into the dark. Revelation is not some mysterious unquestionable propositional knowledge that is made available in an ineffable manner. The word is properly used of those persons and experiences that are particularly transparent to the presence of God, and of the record of those divine encounters. Of course God is always present, just as the laws of nature are always acting; but in the same way that there are particular contrived circumstances (which we call experiments) in which the character of natural law can most readily be discerned, so there have been seminal religious experiences through which God has been most readily perceived. For the Christian, the focus of divine self-disclosure has been in the history of Israel and in the person of Jesus Christ, and what gives the Bible its unique importance and authority is its witness to these events.

The significance of the specific is much higher in theology than in science. Because of the impersonal character of its material (the world as "it"), science is usually able to repeat its phenomena under controllable conditions. That is not always so — cosmology must rest content with the one universe of our observable experience — but the historical sciences tend to lean heavily on the experimental sciences for their interpretative power. Theology is concerned with the personal and, indeed, with transpersonal divine Reality (the world as "thou"). In such a realm of experience, the unique has an indispensable role. It is by no means inconceivable that the fullest knowledge of God was in the possession of a wandering carpenter in a peripheral province of the Roman Empire, far away and long ago.

It is the essence of a rational inquiry to conform its method to the intrinsic nature of the reality encountered. In our investigation of the physical world, we possess the wonderful power of experiment to interrogate that world at will. Once we enter the realm of the personal, testing must give way to trusting. If I am always setting little traps to see if you are my friend, I will, by those very actions, destroy the possibility of real friendship between us. It is a fundamental fact of the spiritual life that "you shall not put the Lord your God to the test." In consequence, there is less unanimity of conclusion to be obtained in these personal matters, as we all know when we compare our judgments of other people's character. What appears generosity to one will seem a spendthrift act to another. Yet these difficulties should not deter us from the delicate but essential task of seeking truth about people and about God.

I belong to the Anglican tradition, which has always believed its theological thinking to require a tripod base: scripture, tradition, and reason. Scripture has an indispensable normative role because it records the foundational experiences through which we believe God has made himself most clearly known. Our knowledge of Jesus Christ as an historical figure is virtually entirely dependent on the documents of the New Testament. Yet those documents are not just plain, matter-of-fact accounts. They are already interpreted. In theology, as in science, we approach experience from a point of view, wearing those "spectacles behind the eyes." That view is not incorrigibly fixed. It can undergo development and correction in the light of continuing experience and further reflection. This is the role of tradition, the record of the insights of the worshiping and believing community. Religion is not something "out there" for our detached intellectual perusal alone. It touches all of what we are, and therefore it must be pursued within a community of relationships. Yet that community is not just engaged in a social conspiracy to see it that way. Like the scientific community, the church is concerned with truth, and in its pursuit the church must be prepared to employ critical reason, the third leg of the theological tripod. As part of that use of reason, theology will need to pay respect to what all other forms of inquiry can tell it about the way things are. Included in that is the need to pay attention to science, whose insights will impose conditions of consonance that theology must take into account. The tone of its discourse about creation has certainly been affected by the realization that the physical world as we know it did not spring into being, ready-made, a few thousand years ago, but it has had a long, evolving history.

One of my favorite quotations is from a twentieth-century Canadian Jesuit, Bernard Lonergan. He worked in the great theological tradition stemming from St. Thomas Aquinas, which sees all search for truth as ultimately the search for God, whether God is known by name or not. Lonergan wrote, "God is the unrestricted act of understanding, the eternal rapture glimpsed in every Archimedean cry of Eureka."[2] That is the true spirit of theology.

2. *The physical world testifies to the Logos.* In chapter 3 I drew attention to the rational beauty, and transparency to our investigation, that is so remarkable a feature disclosed to science in its deeper explorations of the universe. One could interpret the "unreasonable effectiveness" of mathematics in acting as the key to an understanding of the physical world by saying that that world is shot through with signs of mind. To the religious believer that is indeed the case, for it is the Mind of God that is revealed in that wonderful order.

That insight would be an example of theology's ability to answer meta-questions arising from science but going beyond the latter's self-limited power to deal with. My instinct as a scientist is to seek an understanding through and through. That thirst for understanding will not be quenched by science alone. If we are to explain why the reason of our minds so perfectly fits the rational structure of the world, it is likely that the clue will be found in some deeper rationality that embraces both. The rational will of the Creator provides just such an explanation.

I do not present that as a knockdown case for theism. I do not believe that there are any strict proofs either of God's existence or of God's nonexistence. But I do present it as an intellectually satisfying insight. I would not claim that atheism is stupid, merely that it is less comprehensive in its explanatory grasp than is belief in God.

Arguments of this kind have a very long history. In the ancient world they were often expressed in terms of the *Logos,* which is much more than word; it is something like a divine rational order. John's famous prologue speaks of the Word "through whom all things were made and without whom was not anything made that was made." Saint Augustine found that very familiar, but he encountered something entirely new when John went on to make the astonishing Christian claim that "the Word was made flesh and dwelt among us."

3. *The world is a fruitful creation endowed with freedom.* Theology answers the meta-question arising from the insights of the anthropic principle by interpreting the fine-tuning of physical law and circumstance as the fertile endowments given to the universe by a Creator who wills it to be capable of a fruitful history. Indeed, we do not live in "any old world," but in a creation.

So far, so good, but theology has also to reckon with the way in which that potential fertility is made actual. At every stage of cosmic or terrestrial history, it is through the interplay of two opposing tendencies, which in a shorthand sort of way we might call "chance and necessity." By chance I mean just "happenstance," the actual way things turn out to be. There happens to be a genetic mutation that then produces a new possibility for the form life takes. These novel offerings of chance would, however, have no lasting significance if they were not sifted and preserved in a lawfully regular environment. That is what I mean by necessity. Natural selection would not work unless the environmental conditions were relatively stable and the transmission of genetic information from one generation to the next were not reasonably reliable. For creativity, the physical world must be neither too rigid nor too sloppy.

The problem here for theology is to know what to make of the role of chance, with its implication that the history of evolution is contingent and not the unfolding of an inevitable master plan. To some biologists, such as Jacques Monod, the role of chance has meant that ultimately the universe is a tale told by an idiot. A favorite adjective for conveying this message is to call chance "blind."

There is no unique way of going from science to metaphysics, but there is an alternative interpretation available that is more congenial to the religious thinker. It emphasizes in a more even-handed way the twin roles of chance *and* necessity. The God of love will endow his creation with an appropriate measure of freedom. God cannot exert the unrelaxing grip of a cosmic tyrant; rather, God must allow the other truly to be itself. The contingencies of chance are then seen to be reflections of this gift; an evolutionary universe is a creation allowed by its Creator to explore and realize its own God-given potential. But God is not only loving; God is also faithful. God's eternal reliability will find its reflection in the regularity (but not rigidity) of natural law, which makes its indispensable contribution to cosmic fruitfulness. That is how a theologian might read the significance of the interplay of chance and necessity.

It is a very important theological concept to recognize that creation involves God in a voluntary self-limitation as he graciously allows something other than himself to have a genuine life of its own. This insight affords some modest help with the greatest of all theological perplexities — the problem of suffering and evil. It is surely better to have a world of freely choosing beings than a world of totally programmed automata. Yet the necessary cost of the former is the allowing of these free beings to make wrong moral choices. This is in essence the so-called free-will defense in relation to moral evil (the chosen cruelties of humankind). I believe that this needs augmentation by a free-process defense in relation to physical evil (disease and disaster).[3] Austin Farrer once asked, What was God's will in the dreadful disaster of the Lisbon earthquake, which killed fifty thousand people in one day in 1755? His answer, hard but true, was that the elements of the earth's crust should behave in accordance with their nature. They have their due independence also. I believe that God neither wills the act of a murderer nor the incidence of a cancer, but God allows both to happen in a world to which he has given its creaturely independence.

One might say that it is one thing to claim value in allowing moral beings to exercise free choice, but what is the value in allowing tectonic plates to slip? I think that the answer is probably that only a universe that is subject to the free-process defense could be one that could give rise to beings subject to the free-will defense. We have emerged in the history of the physical universe, and although our self-consciousness means that we transcend our origins, yet we are still closely linked in character to the physical world that gave us birth. Its openness is the ground of our freedom.

4. *The open future of the world allows room for God's providential action.* Twentieth-century physics has seen the death of mere mechanism. I indicated in chapter 3 that quantum theory and chaotic dynamics both suggest that we live in a world of true becoming.

The future is not rigidly determined, but its form is contained within certain limits of possibility. Which of these possibilities is actually realized will then depend upon the action of further causal principles that I believe take the form of something like "active information." In this way I picture a possible eventual understanding (still very remote in any detail) of how the mental and the material relate to each other, how my intention of raising my hand is translated into the act of its raising. If this is the right way in which to think about human agency, I think it is also the way in which we can think of divine providential agency as well. The physical world is very much more clouds than clocks, and I imagine God's guiding hand to be at work within the cloudiness of unpredictable open physical process. If that is the case, two things follow. One is that God's action will always be hidden. It will not be demonstrable by experiment, though it may be discernible by faith. The other is that God's providence is conceived as acting within the grain of natural process, not against it. That is to be expected theologically, because the laws of nature are not constraints acting independently of God, but rather, they are expressions of God's will. God cannot act against himself.

Christian theology has to steer a middle course between two unacceptable extremes. God is not a cosmic tyrant who keeps all that happens within his tight control alone. We have already seen that the idea of the gift of creaturely independence is essential if we are to find any answer to the problems of theodicy. Yet God is not to be pictured as a deistic spectator either, simply watching all that happens in indifferent or impotent detachment. In the eighteenth century, deism flourished because the clockwork picture of the physical world then in vogue seemed to leave God with no other role to fulfill. We are delivered from that theological inanity today.

There is, however, a theological consequence of a world of true becoming that may prove less palatable at first encounter. The future is not yet formed; it is not waiting for our arrival, for we make it as we go along. In these circumstances it seems to me to be likely that even God does not know the future. That is no divine imperfection; God knows all that *can* be known, but the future is not yet there to be known. Of course, God will not be caught out by the future, in the sense that God is prepared for it whatever it may be: and I believe God will accomplish his purposes, though by contingent paths.

If this is correct, it has two implications. The first is that, in addition to God's eternal nature, God must also possess a true experience of time. Much modern theology has sought to find ways of speaking of God that assign to the divine nature a temporal/eternal dipolarity. That will not come as a surprise to readers of the Bible, whose God is very much portrayed as One caught up with, and acting through, the history of God's people. The second implication is that creation, in addition to involving a voluntary *kenosis* (emptying) of divine power (in allowing something other than God to exist), also involves a *kenosis* of divine knowledge, in that God does not know beforehand the outcome of a free act or a free process.

5. *Theology will often challenge our commonsense assumptions.*

We saw in chapter 3 that the physical world often behaves in regimes remote from everyday experience, in ways that are counterintuitive to our expectations. If science is often surprising, we may expect that theology will be more so. Clearly, the Infinite is going to elude the grasp of our finite minds. Hence the warnings of apophatic theology that it is easier to say what God is not than what God is. The symbol of Sinai, where God is to be found in clouds and thick darkness, is a powerful and necessary one.

We have to avoid the extreme of cutting down God to our human size, but equally we must avoid the other extreme of a facile invocation of mystery in a lazy substitute for the rigors of theological thought. Paradox is to be embraced only when it is forced upon us by experience. Here the lesson from science is clear and helpful. Nineteenth-century physics established the wave nature of light, but the work of Planck and Einstein in the early years of this century also made it clear that in certain circumstances light behaved as if composed of particles. No progress would have been made by denying either half of this apparently irreconcilable behavior. For many years physicists had to cling to experience without being sure how to make sense of it. Eventually, the discovery of quantum field theory provided an understanding of this strange behavior.

It has been the testimony of the church from the earliest times that its experience of Christ cannot be contained within human language alone, but the church is driven to use divine titles for Christ and to pay him worship. It is profoundly perplexing how both the infinity of God and the finiteness of human nature can be focused on a single figure, but if that is the form reality is found to take (as I believe it is), then the rational response is to wrestle with the paradox and not to dismiss it by a truncated account, reduced to everyday terms alone.

6. *The insights of theology are exciting.* I have already begun to speak of the incarnation, that quintessential Christian ascription of both human and divine status to Jesus Christ. It is a deeply exciting concept that the God who is in so many ways

ineffable and beyond human power to grasp should have acted to make himself known in the plainest possible terms by living the life of a human being. There is a deep human longing to know what God is like, to discover what is the nature of Ultimate Reality. As a Christian I believe that that disclosure has been made in Jesus Christ. Equally exciting is the idea that by sharing in the life of humanity, God in Christ has redeemed that life from its manifest limitation and distortion by sin and that Jesus' resurrection is the ground of the hope of a destiny beyond death in which we all will share. "For as in Adam all die, so also in Christ shall all be made alive" (1 Cor. 15:22). Within the confines of this chapter, I cannot explore these great themes any further, defending their rationality and explaining why I believe in their truth. All I can say is that the possibility that these things might be so is surely the most important matter that we could ever be called upon to investigate.

Another satisfying insight of theology is the way in which it can tie together the diverse layers of our multivalued experience. The physical world, whose rational order is revealed to us by science, is also the carrier of beauty, the arena of moral decision, and the place of religious encounter. It is both significant and puzzling that there is this variety in our experience. The religious believer can perceive the divine unity that underlies and unites this polyvalent diversity: science is exploring the rational order of creation; our aesthetic pleasures are a sharing in God's joy in that creation; our moral intuitions are intimations of God's will; our religious experience is the true meeting with him.

7. *Yet theology is problematic.* It would be disingenuous not to recognize that there are difficulties in accepting a religious account of reality. I want briefly to address the two that I think hold more people back from belief than any others and that are continuing perplexities for those of us who take our stand in the community of faith.

The first is the problem of evil and suffering. I do not need to elaborate; we are all only too aware of it. Does a world with the

Holocaust and the Bangladeshi floods really look like the creation of a loving and almighty God? I have already mentioned the free-will defense and the free-process defense as some kind of philosophical response to these problems. Although I think there is some help to be had there, I would not want to pretend that I believe there is some facile way in which evil and suffering can be explained away. The mystery they represent lies much deeper than can be touched by cerebral argument alone. One of the central reasons I am a Christian is that I believe Christianity does meet the problem of suffering at the most profound level.

The Christian God is not a spectator of suffering, looking down in compassion upon the strange world that he has made. Rather, God is a fellow participant in the bitter history of pain and diminishment. The Christian believes that in the cross of Christ, in the darkness and dereliction of Calvary, we see God himself stretching out his arms to embrace the suffering of the world. God accepts being impaled upon the contradictions of creation, and by that acceptance God offers us the hope of a victory over those contradictions. It is a profoundly mysterious and profoundly moving insight that the Christian God is the Crucified God.[4]

The second great problem for religious belief lies in its diversity. If you were to stop a suitable person in the street in Toronto or Delhi or Tokyo and ask him or her what matter is made of, in each of those cities you would receive the same answer — quarks and gluons and electrons. There is a universality of agreement in science that is impressive, and it has proved to be exportable throughout the world. If you were to stop three people in the street in those three cities and ask them the religious question regarding the nature of Ultimate Reality, the chances are that you would receive three different answers. What are we to make of the variety and stability of the world's great religious traditions and their incompatibility with each other? Does it not encourage the view that science deals with a public world of fact, whereas religion is concerned with a private world of opinion? We may respect each other's religious opinion, but are they more than "true for me" or "true for you," rather than being plain "true," pure and simple?

I am not really interested in things that are just true for me. My quest is for truth, not just a congenial manner of speaking. How then can I understand this problem of the variety of religious belief? I offer three comments. The first is that I believe each tradition contains truth about its encounter with a divine reality. God has not left himself without witness in any age or place. The traditions do not all say the same thing, but they are clearly all concerned with the same spiritual dimension of human experience. Second, because the infinite God must veil his presence from finite beings, the divine light will always be refracted by the cultural prisms of humankind. Here is some kind of clue to the phenomenon of diversity, though I cannot claim that I believe it explains the whole of that diversity. Third, whatever respect I rightly accord to my friends in other traditions, I must hold firm, persistently but humbly, to my Christian belief that God has made himself uniquely known in Jesus Christ. Many puzzles remain. I think that the interrelationship of the world's religions is one of the most urgent and most difficult theological problems that we face today.

8. *Theology has things to say to science.* Religion cannot dictate the scientific program of investigation nor prescribe what the results of those investigations will be. There is a due autonomy on the part of science that theology must respect. Yet that does not mean that there are not insights from theology that will complement and complete the insights of a science whose success stems, partly at least, from the self-restricted modesty of its ambitions. There are many questions that are meaningful to ask and necessary to address with which science is powerless to deal. Some of these are those meta-questions, such as the significance of the deep intelligibility of the physical world and of its finely tuned anthropic fruitfulness, which we have already considered. Because theology aims to speak of God, it must have things to say that are relevant to all that is, for nothing exists except by God's will. In that sense, theology is still

the "Queen of Sciences," not because it can lord it over other forms of rational inquiry but because it can take the results of those inquiries and embed them in the most profound and comprehensive matrix of understanding. However satisfying science can be, its impersonal approach will never touch more than the periphery of our human experience. All those things that touch us in our inner being lie beyond its grasp. Deep within us is an intuition of hope and human significance, despite the manifest transience of life in this world. Is there a purpose at work in the history of the universe? Is something really happening in what is going on? Is there a destiny awaiting us beyond our death? These are religious questions, and the search for their answers is part of the quest for truth. I believe that both science and theology are to be taken with the utmost seriousness and that they are cousinly partners in that necessary search for the fullest possible understanding.

– Five –

CREATION

THE CENTRAL RELIGIOUS QUESTION is the question of truth. Religious affirmations may guide us in life and sustain us at death, but they can properly do so only if they are affirmations of the truth. My experience as a scientist and my experience as a clergyman and would-be theologian have this in common: they are both concerned with attempts to discern what is the case. In this chapter and the two that follow, I want to explore as candidly as I can the motivation there might be for three great affirmations of Christian belief: (1) that the physical world is a creation sustained by the will of God and that its history contains the unfolding of God's purpose; (2) that God interacts with his creatures, who are the objects of his providential care; and (3) that Jesus was raised from the dead the first Easter day by a great divine act that is the guarantee and foretaste of a destiny beyond death for all of us.

One could hardly think of three more exciting or significant claims to make. If these affirmations are actually true, it is of the highest importance that we should come to know that this is so. Yet they are also affirmations that run counter to the understandings and expectations of the secular age in which we live. Are they profound insights that we are in danger of losing, or are they remnants of an outdated and discredited worldview that we cannot dispose of too soon? I believe they are the former, and in what follows I will seek to defend that belief. You will not expect me to establish these matters beyond a peradventure; no one in this area of human discourse has access to knockdown argument, whether this stance is one of belief or one of disbelief. You will, however, rightly expect me to offer you reasons for my affirmations. They must be motivated by a consideration of the evidence and not presented as a form of unquestionable knowledge made available by some ineffable process of revelation. In my consideration of the first two questions — creation and providence — I will be assisted by some insights suggested by the discoveries of modern science. I believe that our contemporary understanding of the physical universe is more hospitable to an ample metaphysical interpretation than has been recognized by those who pursue a narrow and crass reductionism. The resurrection is a unique event that cannot gain much illumination from the general deliverances of science, but I will carry to its discussion those evidence-based habits of rational inquiry that my scientific career has inculcated in me.

•

Astronomy and cosmology catch the public imagination in a way that no other branches of science do. Witness the excitement about the "cosmic ripples" discerned by the COBE satellite and the astonishing multimillion sales of Stephen Hawking's *Brief History of Time*. There is more to this concern than a simple curiosity induced by looking up at the starry heavens on a clear night. Beneath the scientific interest there lies an archetypal longing to know whence we came and whither we are going. Is this vast universe something that just happened to be, or is there a meaning and a purpose within its story? Is it possible that we are, in fact, part of a *creation* ?

That, of course, is a religious question. Science, by its self-denying modesty of ambition, which is also the enabler of its great but limited success, has foresworn the attempt to address wider questions of meaning and purpose and confines itself to prosaic issues of process, the causal sequences by which things happen. Scientists themselves have been less austere in practice than their ostensible principles would require them to be. Although officially they foreswear metaphysics, covertly they love it and lace their popular writings with *obiter dicta* of that kind. Hence the claims either to discern the mind of God or to dispose of God altogether. I am not against such metaphysical indulgences, for it seems to me quite impossible to live without them in one form or another. It belongs to our humanity to wrestle with questions of significance and purpose that, contrary to the claims of some that they are meaningless issues, are in fact so meaningful for us that they insistently clamor to be addressed. I am simply eager that we should be clear in our minds about what is the character of the discourse in which we are engaged and what authority and success in one kind of inquiry should not be invoked to settle illegitimately issues in a different domain of discussion.

Physics and metaphysics are two distinct disciplines, but they must bear some consonant relationship to each other. Neither directly entails the other — so that philosophy or theology cannot dictate to science what the physical world is actually like, nor can science foreclose the discussion of wider issues beyond its narrow ken — but there is an inescapable interaction between the two. Let me put the point in simple terms, at the same time transposing it into a religious mode. It is a somewhat crude, but not altogether misleading, remark to say that science is concerned with answering the question *How?* and theology is concerned with answering the question *Why?* Now these are certainly distinct questions, and we are familiar with the fact that one can ask and answer both questions about the same event: the kettle is boiling because the burning gas heats the water *and* because I want to make a cup of tea. Yet there must be an appropriateness between the two answers proffered that makes them mutually consistent. If I say that my purpose is to make a cup of tea and the way I am going to do so is by putting the kettle in the refrigerator rather than on the gas, you will rightly doubt the genuineness of my stated intention.

Therefore there is some intellectual traffic between science and theology on the issue of creation, but it is of a subtle and discrete kind. We do not expect the universe to be full of objects stamped "Made by God," but if there is a mind and purposive will behind cosmic history — and that is the substance of the claim that the universe is a creation — then we might (indeed we must) look for hints arising from the scientific story that are at least consonant with such a metaphysical claim. Equally, there may be aspects of the traditional theological story that will need revision or excision in the light of what we have learned from science. In the past, the Judeo-Christian tradition frequently used a literal interpretation of Genesis 3 to encourage an understanding in which the present flawedness of human nature and the marredness of the physical world were interpreted as following upon a period of paradisal perfection that was brought to an end by a disastrous ancestral act. Whatever meaning the deep myth of the Fall has for us today, it cannot play that etiological role of accounting for present ills as arising from a previous act of degeneration. Cosmic history has been the weaving of a seamless evolutionary web, and death has always been the necessary price of new life. The need for consonance with the findings of science can be a healthy corrective for theology, whose persistent temptation is to indulge in ungrounded speculation.

What theology can do for science is to provide answers to those meta-questions that arise from science but go beyond what science itself can answer. The role of theology as providing the ultimate quenching of the thirst for an understanding through and through is one that has been particularly stressed in the tradition stemming from Thomas Aquinas.

With these thoughts in mind, let us consider the question of the credibility of a doctrine of creation in this scientific age.

ORIGINS

Perhaps no subject has given rise to more confusion on the interrelationship of science and theology than the question of how things began. It has often erroneously been supposed that the Christian doctrine of creation is principally concerned with initiation, with the primary instant. To think that is to confuse Christianity with deism. The doctrine of creation is concerned, not just with what God did, but with what God is doing; its subject is ontological origin, not temporal beginning. Its central assertion is that the universe, at every instant of its existence, is held in being by the will of God. God is as much the Creator today as God was fifteen billion years ago. God's role is not to light the blue touch paper of the Big Bang and then retire.

Two consequences follow. The first is that if physical cosmology delivers us a datable moment when the universe as we know it sprang forth from the Big Bang, that is scientifically very interesting but theologically neutral. There never was a theological stake in preferring Big Bang cosmology to steady state cosmology. Second, and conversely, if physical cosmology were to abolish a datable beginning for the world, no great theological upheaval would follow. Stephen Hawking has proposed a highly speculative, but just conceivably correct, quantum cosmology in which the universe is a kind of fuzzy space-time egg with no sharp beginning. He says, "If the universe is really completely self-contained, having no boundary or edge, it would have neither beginning nor end; it would simply be. What place then for a creator?" It is theologically naive to give any other answer than "every place" — as the ordainer and sustainer of the space-time egg. God is not a God of the Edges, with a vested interest in boundaries. In fact, there is a contemporary current of thought in theology, particularly associated with Jürgen Moltmann, that stresses the gift of a genuine "otherness" made by a loving Creator to the creation, and that would find very appropriate physical realization in a universe "really completely self-contained." If there are problems for Christian theology in cosmological thought, they lie, not in questions of origins, but in the question of the end.

THE END

Cosmologists not only peer into the past; they also attempt to discern the future. On the grandest scale, the history of the universe is a tug-of-war between two opposing principles: the explosion of the Big Bang, throwing matter apart; and the pull of gravity, drawing matter together. They are very evenly balanced, and we do not know which will win. Accordingly, we have to consider two alternative scenarios for the universe's future. If expansion wins, the galaxies will continue to fly apart forever. Within themselves, gravity will certainly win, and they will condense into gigantic black holes, eventually decaying into low-grade radiation. That way lies cosmic death. The alternative scenario presents no more cheerful a prospect. If gravity wins, the present expansion will one day be halted and reversed. What began with the Big Bang will end with the Big Crunch, as the universe falls back into a singular cosmic melting pot. That way lies collapse.

On the face of it, the ultimate prospects for the universe are bleak. What does that imply for theology's claim that there is a purpose at work in the world, so central to the idea of creation? Christian orthodoxy has never subscribed to an evolutionary optimism that expects a total fulfillment of divine purpose to be brought about within the flux of present physical process. If there is a true and lasting hope — and it is a deep human intuition that there is such a hope — then it can rest only in the eternal mercy and faithfulness of God. Christians have that hope for themselves (our bodies, after all, will decay on a timescale of tens of years) in their assertion of a destiny beyond death, and they can believe it as well for the whole universe (whose decay will be on a timescale of tens of billions of years).

They need to embrace a cosmic hope as well as a personal hope, for it would be far too anthropocentric simply to regard this vast universe as being of concern to God only as the backdrop for a human drama that has just started after an overture lasting fifteen billion years. It is, of course, beyond our feeble powers of imagination to conceive what that act of cosmic redemption will be like, but if there is a true hope, it lies in God and not in physics.

Some of those unable to embrace a hope arising from casting oneself on divine faithfulness have engaged in ingenious speculation about whether there might nevertheless be some form of adequate fulfillment attainable within physical process. As cosmic circumstances change radically within the universe's evolving history, the embodiment of intelligence would have to adapt itself to what is going on. Carbon-based life is certainly condemned to extinction, and it would have to give way to successors that it had itself produced by conscious design. There might eventually be "thinking plasmas," engineered by their predecessors, in the great chain of intelligent being. In this way, even within the chronologically finite history of a collapsing universe, there might be such rapidly accelerating processing of information that a kind of infinite "psychological" history would be able to unfold. This kind of "physical eschatology" has been particularly pursued by Frank Tipler. He exhibits great speculative ingenuity, but it seems to me that it is a thin and abstract hope that these fast-racing cosmic computers would fulfill. Tipler's "physical eschatology" is a kind of cosmic Tower of Babel. In contrast, the Christian hope is that nothing of individual and particular good is ever lost in the Lord and that an unending exploration of the riches of the divine life awaits us.

So far I have been considering the constraints that scientific knowledge lays upon theological thinking. Let us now consider two of the meta-questions arising from science that seem to call for an answer that a doctrine of creation can most fittingly provide.

INTELLIGIBILITY

One of the most striking features of the physical world is its rational transparency to us. We have come to take it for granted that we can understand the universe, but it is surely a highly significant fact about it that this is the case. Einstein once said that the only incomprehensible thing about the universe is that it is comprehensible. He was referring to what another famous physicist, Eugene Wigner, in a memorable phrase, called "the unreasonable effectiveness of mathematics." Time and again we have found that the physical theories that fit the facts are characterized in their formulation by that unmistakable quality of mathematical beauty. It is an actual technique in fundamental physics to seek theories endowed with mathematical economy and elegance in the (historically justified) expectation that they will be the ones that describe the way the world actually is. There is a marvelous relationship between the workings of our minds (the mathematical reason within) and the workings of the physical world (the scientific reason without). Up to a point the need to survive in the evolutionary struggle provides an explanation of why this is so. If our thoughts did not match in some degree the world around us, we would all have perished. But that can apply only to the relation of everyday experience (the world of rocks and trees), to everyday thinking (counting and simple geometry). Wigner was not talking about anything as banal as that. He had in mind such things as the counterintuitive quantum world, whose strangeness is made sense of in terms of highly abstract mathematical entities. It is hard to believe that the ability to understand that strange, unpicturable, quantum world is just a spin-off from evolutionary competition; that Dirac's ability to discover quantum field theory was a consequence of our ancestors having had to dodge saber-toothed tigers.

Science does not explain the mathematical intelligibility of the physical world, for it is part of science's founding faith that this is so. We can always decline to put the question, shrug our shoulders, and say, "That's the way it is, and good luck for you mathematical chaps." It goes against the grain for a scientist to be so intellectually lazy. The meta-question of the unreasonable effectiveness of mathematics insists on being answered. A coherent and elegant explanation would lie in the theological claim that the reason within and the reason without are linked together by their common origin in the rationality of the Creator. The physical universe in its rational beauty and transparency seems shot through with signs of mind. That is indeed so, says the theist, for it is God's mind that lies behind its rational beauty. I do not offer this as a knockdown argument for theism — there are no such arguments, either for or against — but as a satisfying insight that finds a consistent place in a theistic view of the universe.

THE ANTHROPIC PRINCIPLE

In the last thirty years or so, scientists have been led to the conclusion that a universe that is fruitful in evolving complexity out of simplicity — to the degree that an almost homogeneous ball of energy becomes, after fifteen billion years, a home for self-conscious beings — is not in scientific terms "any old world," but rather one that is special in the finely tuned balance of its laws. Notice that we are referring here, not to particular events within cosmic history, but to those natural laws that are the necessary basis for any cosmic history.

Although it would be easy to devote a chapter solely to this theme, I must be content to give only a few examples. One relates to the stars. A fruitful universe must contain stars and of the right kind, for stars are not only energy sources but also the nuclear furnaces in which the elements essential for life are made. The early universe was so simple that it could generate only the simplest elements, hydrogen and helium. Life needs a richer chemistry than they can provide. In particular, it needs the chemistry of carbon, with its aptness to produce long chain molecules. Every atom of carbon in our bodies was once inside a star, we are all made from the ashes of dead stars. In order to have stars that are steadily burning for long periods, which can make all the necessary elements in usable abundances and which, at least in some cases, explode as supernovae so as to make these elements available in the environment of a subsequent planet, there has to be a precise balance between the strengths of the fundamental forces of nature. Only a small shift from that balance would destroy the possibility of life in the universe.

My second example refers to something we often feel is rather daunting — the vast size of the universe. Our sun is an ordinary star among the hundred thousand million stars of our galaxy, the Milky Way. And the Milky Way is just an ordinary galaxy among the hundred thousand million galaxies of the observable universe. We may find that immensity to be a rather chilling thought. We should not do so, however, for if all those trillions of stars were not there, neither would we be here to be upset at the thought of them! We now understand that there is a necessary connection between how big the universe is and how long it lasts. A universe that is smaller than ours would not have survived for the fifteen billion years or so needed to make men and women; it is a process that cannot be hurried.

Thus we see that a universe capable of being anthropically fruitful is a very special kind of universe — one in a trillion, one might say. Once we understand this, then a meta-question arises regarding why things are this special way. If they were not, we would not be here to worry about them, but it does not seem just enough to say, "We're here because we're here," and leave it at that. Instead, there is the hint of an amazing anti-Copernican revolution. We do not live at the center of the universe, but it does look as though the very fabric of the cosmos has been given a character that is required if the emergence of beings like us is to be a possibility. There seems to be the chance of a revised and revived argument from design — not ap-

pealing to Paley's Cosmic Craftsman working within physical
process (which process science explains in a way not requir-
ing intervention by such a God of the Gaps) — but appealing
to a cosmic planner who has endowed the world with a potentiality implanted within the delicate balance of the laws of
nature themselves, which laws science cannot explain because
it assumes them as the basis for its explanation of the process.
In short, the claim would be that the universe is indeed not
"any old world" but the carefully calculated construct of its
Creator.

It is necessary to consider some arguments advanced in
rebuttal of such a claim:

1. Perhaps there are lots and lots of different universes, each
with its law and circumstance. In that case, it would be no
more surprising that one of them fulfilled the anthropic con-
dition than it would be to find an almost spherical pebble if
one had sorted over a million specimens in the first place. That
would be the particular universe that we live in because we
could not turn up anywhere else. This "portfolio of universes"
approach has been quite popular in one way or another. It can
be tricked out in various scientific-sounding ways, but it seems
to me not to be a scientific proposal (for scientifically, we only
have adequate motivation to speak of this particular universe
of our actual physical experience); rather, it is a metaphysical
guess. Its interest lies in the fact that by making such guesses
people indicate clearly that they feel there is really something
calling for an explanation. To my mind, a metaphysical speculation of equal coherence and greater economy is that there
is just one universe, anthropically finely tuned because it is
the creation of a Creator who wills it to be capable of fruitful process. Again, I present that as a proffered insight, not a
knockdown argument.

2. The most interesting counter-argument is that the anthropic principle is the fruit of limited imagination, for its
questions of balance center around the conditions necessary to
ensure the eventual development of carbon-based life. Perhaps

intelligence and self-consciousness could have totally different embodiments, not based on carbon chemistry — a thinking plasma perhaps, like Fred Hoyle's Black Cloud. Perhaps all universes (or a great many) are capable of producing their own idiosyncratic forms of "life." Perhaps..., but those who speak this way are drawing a very large intellectual blank check on an unknown account. The only form of intelligent and self-conscious life that we know about is carbon based. When one considers the physical complexity of the human brain (far and away the most intricately interconnected physical system we have ever encountered), it is difficult not to believe that this degree of structure is necessary as the physical substrate sustaining self-consciousness, and it is very hard to believe that there are many radically different ways of realizing naturally such a necessary complexity. Our knowledge of how brain and mind relate is so pitifully rudimentary that no one can be dogmatic about what is possible, but I regard it as wholly reasonable not to entertain seriously this ground for rebutting the claim of anthropic significance.

Having said all that, I do not doubt that some anthropic "coincidences" that now seem special may be found to result from other deeper linkages. (So-called inflationary cosmology, a kind of early "boiling" of space has already provided one possible example of how this might happen, in relation to the anthropic requirement that cosmic expansion and gravitational attraction must be very evenly balanced in a fruitful universe, which must neither become too dilute nor suffer too prompt collapse.) However, I think it is entirely reasonable to expect that there would still be some things distinctly and minutely particular about a world capable of producing men and women. I therefore conclude that there is a meta-question arising from anthropic principle considerations to which theism provides a persuasive, but not logically coercive answer.

So far so good, as far as the religious believer is concerned, but we must go on to inquire how exactly it is that an anthropically finely tuned universe is able actually to realize its inherent fruitfulness. The answer can be expressed in summary terms by acknowledging that evolving complexity comes about through the interplay of two opposing tendencies encapsulated in the slogan "Chance and Necessity."

CHANCE AND NECESSITY

As we survey the cosmic process that has carried the universe from initial simplicity to present differentiated richness, at every stage the realization of anthropic potentiality has depended upon an interplay of two opposing tendencies that we can conveniently summarize in epigrammatic form as "chance" and "necessity." By chance I mean just happenstance, the ways things come together in an essentially uncorrelated sequence of occurrences: a fluctuation produces a little more primeval matter here than there; a genetic mutation produces a new characteristic of animal life. Through such novel offerings of chance there came about the condensation of the galaxies and the origin of new species. Yet for those things to happen also required the presence of lawful necessity to preserve and sift the novelty provided: gravity enhancing the matter fluctuation; evolutionary biology operating within a stable, and so effectively selective, environment, transmitting genetic information with tolerable accuracy from one generation to another.

Some have felt that the role assigned to chance subverts religious claims of a purpose at work. After all, what will eventually happen is not foreseeable at the beginning. The universe is given something of the air of a game of cosmic roulette. With characteristic Gallic rhetoric, Jacques Monod spoke of "pure chance, absolutely free but blind, at the base of the stupendous edifice of evolution." For him the role of chance turned the universe's history into a tale told by an idiot.

At times one feels that Monod lost sight of the indispensable, complementary role of necessity, with its implications of finely tuned anthropic law. If one attempts a more evenhanded evaluation of the interplay of chance and necessity, then an alternative metaphysical interpretation becomes possible that is, in my view, fully consonant with a doctrine of creation.

The Christian God is both loving and faithful. The gift of the God of love to his creation will surely be freedom. God will prove to be no cosmic tyrant, holding all in tight control. Yet freedom by itself can only too readily degenerate into license and chaos. The gift of the God of faithfulness will surely be reliability. God will prove to be no cosmic lord of misrule. Yet reliability by itself can all too readily degenerate into an iron rigidity. We may expect the creation of the God who is both loving and faithful to display characteristics of both openness and regularity, such as are in fact reflected in the physical interplay of chance and necessity in the process of the world. That is the divinely ordained way in which the creation is allowed to make itself.

A doctrine of creation of this open yet regular kind can indeed be found in contemporary Christian theology, not only in the writings of Moltmann, to which I referred earlier, but also in the work of the English theologian W. H. Vanstone. He is motivated, not by acquaintance with the scientific story, but by meditation on the necessary precariousness and value of any act of creativity by love. This leads him to write, "If the creation is the work of love, then its shape cannot be predetermined by the Creator, nor its triumph foreknown: it is the realization of vision, but of vision which is discovered only through its own realization." Such an account is perfectly consonant with the scientific insight of the realization of anthropic fruitfulness through the shuffling explorations of happenstance.

This understanding can afford us some help with what is for theology the most painful of its difficulties. I refer, of course, to the problem of evil.

THE PROBLEM OF EVIL

Does the universe really look like the creation of a good and powerful God? Some modest help with the question of moral evil (the chosen cruelties of humankind) is given by the so-called free-will defense. It asserts that a world of freely choosing beings is better than a world of perfectly programmed automata, however destructive some of those choices may prove to be. Our instinctive recoil from coercive measures, such as the castration of persistent sex offenders, shows us that we accord some force to this insight. However, it leaves untouched the problem of physical evil (disease and disaster). I believe this needs what I have called the free-process defense, appealing to the divine gift of freedom to all of God's creation, not just to humankind alone. Austin Farrer once asked himself what was God's will in the Lisbon earthquake. His answer, hard but true, was that the elements of the earth's crust should act in accordance with their nature. God wills neither the act of a murderer nor the incidence of cancer, but allows both to happen in a world to which he has granted the freedom to be itself.

One might counter by saying that, though freedom is necessary for moral beings to exist, what is the value in allowing tectonic plates to slip as they please? I suspect that the answer lies in our deep embedding in the natural world that has given birth to humankind. Only a universe to which the free-process defense applied would be able to give rise to beings to whom the free-will defense would be applicable.

I do not pretend that these considerations remove the deep mystery of the existence of suffering and evil in the created order, though they seek to show that it is not gratuitous. One of my central reasons for being a Christian is that the Christian God is not a benevolent spectator, looking down compassionately on his so often strange creation. The Christian God is also a fellow participant in its suffering, for we believe that in the darkness and dereliction of the cross of Christ we see God opening his arms to embrace the bitterness of the world.

I would like to end this chapter by quoting something I wrote in my book *Science and Creation* concerning the mutual relationship of science and theology.

> Einstein once said, "Religion without science is blind. Science without religion is lame." His instinct that they need each other was right, though I would not describe their separate shortcomings in quite the terms he chose. Rather I would say, "Religion without science is confined; it fails to be completely open to reality. Science without religion is incomplete; it fails to attain the deepest possible understanding." The remarkable insights that science affords us into the intelligible workings of the world cry out for an explanation more profound than that which it itself can provide. Religion, if it is to take seriously its claim that the world is the creation of God, must be humble enough to learn from science what that world is actually like. The dialogue between them can only be mutually enriching.

Part of that dialogue is the interplay of scientific and religious insight in which we seek to understand the universe as creation.

– Six –

PROVIDENCE

IN CHAPTER 5 I described a physical world that is rationally beautiful and whose history has been astonishingly fruitful. I claimed that these scientific insights were consonant with the religious understanding that the universe is a creation, the expression of the divine mind and purpose. If you grant me all that, my assertions would still fall short of the Christian claim that the One whose will is thus expressed is most fittingly to be spoken of in personal terms. Here was the sticking point for Einstein, as it is for many other scientists. He was impressed by the universe's wonderful order and liked to use God as a symbol for it (referring to God in comradely terms as "the Old One"), but he could not believe in a God who acts, not just in the single great act of holding the world in being, but in some causal way within cosmic history, bringing about things that would not have happened without divine interaction. My question now is, Is such a idea of God's action a coherent possibility for those of us who live in a scientific age?

After all, science discerns a universe that is regular in its operation, and there is no doubt that this makes the question of divine agency one that may seem difficult for us to answer positively. Previous generations might pray for rain in times of drought without uneasiness, but "amen" may well stick in many throats if such prayers are offered in church today. Does not the weather just *happen*?

Yet the God of Christian theology is a *personal* God. We recognize that human language applied to the divine nature must be being used in some stretched or analogical sense; but if personal language about God is to mean anything at all, it must surely mean that God does particular things in particular circumstances. God is to be addressed as "Father" and not as "Force." Thus a great deal is at stake for Christian theology (and, I think, for that of Judaism and Islam too) in seeing whether it is possible, all the difficulties notwithstanding, to answer yes to my question while still maintaining one's scientific integrity.

One might think that one could cut the Gordian knot of theological perplexity by appealing to the omnipotence of God. Can God not do what he likes? It is important to recognize what is meant by speaking of God as "almighty." God can do what he likes, but God wills only *what is in accordance with his nature.* The very last thing that the utterly consistent and rational God can be is a kind of capricious celestial conjurer. Love works by process, respectful of the other's independence and integrity, and not by overruling magic. That is God's relationship with his creation, to which he has given the gracious gift of being itself. Those very laws of nature, whose regularities are discerned by science, are understood by the theologian to be willed by God and to reflect God's continuing faithfulness. God cannot work against the laws of nature, for that would be for God to work against himself. If God acts in the world, his action will be within the grain of the universe and not against it. God cannot deny himself. Of course, consistency is not a dreary uniformity. In unprecedented circumstances, totally unexpected things may happen, giving rise to those events that, because of their surprising character, we might call miracles. Such occurrences are to be understood as signs of a deeper divine rationality than we had previously apprehended, just as unexpected physical phenomena, such as superconductivity, are signs of deeper consequences of the laws of physics than we had previously understood.

If God works within the grain of nature, we have to ask whether that grain is in fact sufficiently open to contain the possibility for such particular divine activity? In a mechanical universe, such as people in the eighteenth and nineteenth centuries conceived the world to be, that could scarcely be the case. If the cosmos were a gigantic piece of clockwork, then the only role for God would be the deistic one of the great clockmaker who constructed the machinery, wound it up, and now just lets it tick away. We have always, in fact, known that mechanical picture to be inadequate to our experience, for we have always known, as surely as we know anything at all, that we are not pieces of elaborate clockwork. People might write books with titles like "Man the Machine," but those who did so took their own writings more seriously than would be appropriate for the scribblings of an automaton.

Twentieth-century science has seen the death of a merely mechanical view of the universe. Two blows have delivered it the coup de grâce. The first was the discovery of quantum theory, the astonishing fact that the physical world is cloudy and fitful at its subatomic roots. The quantum world is unpicturable and unpredictable in detailed behavior. Fascinating though this discovery is — and I have spent the greater part of my adult life working in quantum physics — I do not think it is of the highest significance for our topic. When we consider providence, we are talking about events in the everyday world that involve the behavior of trillions of atoms. Although each atomic event has some degree of randomness in it, the combination of a very large number of such events can, and usually does, produce an overall pattern of great reliability. This is the same principle as that on which life insurance offices work. They do not know when you will die, but the actuaries have a sufficiently good idea of how many people in your cohort will die in the next few years to enable the offices to make money, provided they insure enough people. In the same way, unpredictable microscopic events yield by their sum reliable macroscopic behavior. I doubt whether God interacts with the world by scrabbling around at its subatomic roots.

Much more significant for our present purpose is a most surprising discovery of twentieth-century science that has been widely appreciated only within the last thirty years. It relates to classical physics, the physics of the everyday world. This discovery deals with ideas that would have been familiar to Sir Isaac Newton but shows that they have consequences that would have surprised (and interested) him very much. Those of us who learned about Newtonian physics did so by considering certain simple systems, such as the steadily ticking pendulum. These systems are tame and robust. By that I mean that if you disturb them a little, the consequence for their behavior is correspondingly slight. They are predictable and controllable. We thought that the everyday physical world was like that — that it was mechanical in its nature. But now we have discovered that, though there are clocks in the Newtonian world, most of it is made of clouds. In other words, the world is made up of systems that are so exquisitely sensitive to circumstance that the smallest disturbance will produce large and ever-growing changes in their behavior. It will not surprise you to learn that this behavior came to light in a literally cloudy subject. Ed Lorenz was trying to model the behavior of the earth's weather systems. To his intense surprise he found that the smallest variation in the input to his equations produced exponentiatingly large deviations in the behavior of his solutions. This is called the "butterfly effect:" a butterfly stirring the air with its wings in the African jungle today will have consequences for the storm systems over Boston within three weeks. Because we cannot possibly know about all those African butterflies, detailed long-term weather forecasting is never going to work!

This astonishing discovery is so important that I would like to explain it in a bit more detail. For my example, I will take the air in a room. It consists of lots of little molecules buzzing around. They are not quite miniature billiard balls, but when they collide with each other they behave in the same way that billiard balls do. The molecules are fast moving and fairly close together, so that collisions are frequent. In fact, in only 10^{-10} seconds (one ten thousand millionth of a second) each molecule has on average about fifty collisions with its neighbors. We now pose the question, How accurately must we know the circumstances of one of these molecules at the beginning if we are to know with tolerable accuracy in which direction it will be moving 10^{-10} seconds later? The calculation is straightforward. Newton himself solved the problem of how two balls separate after a collision. The solution is determined exactly by his equations, but the angle at which the balls separate depends very sensitively on the precise angle at which they collided. Anyone who has played pool will know that a small error in cuing the ball produces a large and frustrating error in the subsequent motion after impact. That is so for one collision. If we have fifty successive collisions, these uncertainties mount up rapidly; in fact, they exponentiate. Taking that into account, we reach the following astonishing conclusion: we will make a serious error in our prediction if we have failed to take into account an electron (the smallest particle of matter) at the edge of the observable universe (the furthest distance away) interacting with the air molecules in the room through gravity (the weakest of the fundamental forces of nature). So even as simple a system as air in so short a time as the ten thousand millionth of a second cannot have its detailed behavior worked out without, literally, universal knowledge of all that is happening. Here is a cosmic butterfly effect with a vengeance! Because we cannot possibly know about all those electrons in the most distant galaxies, we have in the air in a room a system that is intrinsically unpredictable. It is also intrinsically unisolatable, sensitive to all that happens in the world around it.

The discovery of the widespread existence of these incredibly sensitive systems is called the theory of chaos. The name is not particularly aptly chosen, for their behavior is not completely random, but it has about it a kind of ordered disorder; there is a pattern to its haphazardness. Chaos theory is an oxymoronic sort of subject. I cannot go into detail about strange attractors and the like, because I want to ask what significance we should attribute to this discovery. What all can agree on is that these systems are unpredictable in behavior and unisolatable in their character because of their extreme vulnerability to any alteration in circumstance. Yet the paradox is that the apparently random behavior that follows from this sensitivity arises from the solution of completely *deterministic* equations. Which are we to take the more seriously, the behavior or the equations?

One could put the issue this way. The property of unpredictability relates to epistemology, what we can *know* about these systems. In fact, we cannot know in detail what their future behavior will be. Is that to be interpreted simply as a matter of ignorance, or is it a pointer to there being an actual openness about the future for such systems? The latter claim would be concerned with ontology, what is actually the case.

Scientists are instinctive realists. That is to say, they believe that what we can or cannot know is a reliable guide to what is indeed the case. Their motto is "Epistemology Models Ontology." I am proud to wear from time to time a sweatshirt my wife gave me with that stirring slogan emblazoned upon it.

You can see how that works by recalling a famous episode in the history of quantum theory. Heisenberg showed that for a quantum entity such as an electron one could not simultaneously know where it was and what it was doing. His analysis proceeded by showing that position and momentum could not both be measured at the same time with arbitrary degrees of accuracy. In other words, his conclusion was initially concerned with epistemology, what could be known about electrons. Yet within a short time, he and almost all other physicists were interpreting the uncertainty principle, not as a principle of ignorance (epistemology), but as a principle of indeterminacy (ontology). If you could not establish the values of both position and momentum, then an electron did not actually possess definite values of those two quantities. Epistemology models ontology!

In a similar way, I want to take the hint from chaos theory and draw from it the ontological conclusion that the physical world, even at the everyday level, is something more subtle and supple than a merely mechanical universe. Added confidence in this strategy arises from the recognition that it thereby begins to describe a world of which we can conceive ourselves as inhabitants. That is a gain for *physics*. I do not for one moment suppose that we did not know ourselves not to be automata till chaotic dynamics came along to assure us that this is so. It is fundamental to all human rational inquiry that we are more than machines. If we were merely computers made of meat, what would validate the programs running in our brains? Doubtless, evolutionary pressures would ensure a certain rough-and-ready adequacy to deal with everyday experience relevant to survival, but the subtlety and capacious grasp of the human intellect vastly exceeds anything that could be justified in that way. Those who affirm a physical reductionist view of humanity saw off the rational branch on which they need to sit while framing their argument.

The present working-out of this open metaphysical picture is necessarily tentative. I believe it will concern us for a very long time to come. I have made various essays in that direction in my writings and can now only sketch the lines of thought involved. The first question is what one makes of the *deterministic* equations from which the theory of chaos began. I believe that they must be treated as *approximations* to a more supple reality, approximations that arise when we treat the parts making up these complex systems as if their behavior could be discussed in separation from the environment that surrounds them. Remember that exquisitely sensitive systems are in fact intrinsically unisolatable, even if, for our convenience, we try to treat them as detachable from their surroundings.

In fact, there is much in modern physics that resists a particulate, reductionist conception of reality. The universe fights back against such treatment and reasserts a need for holism. Even the atomic world cannot adequately be discussed atomistically. The mysterious quantum mechanical "togetherness-in-separation" — discovered by Einstein, Rosen, and Podolsky, and confirmed experimentally by Alain Aspect — by which two electrons, once they have interacted, retain the power to influence each other instantaneously, however far apart they separate, shows that this is so.

To say that the future is open is not to imply that it comes about as the result of some whimsical lottery. Rather, it means that a bottom-up description in terms of isolatable parts will only partly prescribe what will occur (there is structure in chaotic systems, but not a rigid uniqueness of behavior) and that the consequent openness of grain toward the future will give space for the operation of additional causal principles of a holistic, or top-down character in bringing about what actually happens. When one thinks about what form these principles might take, one sees that the character of their operation is what might be called, in a vague but suggestive phrase, "active information." By that I mean that the bottom-up description takes care of questions of energetic interchange between constituents, but in a way that leaves room for additional "pattern-forming" agency within the range of possibility left open in the terms of the bottom-up description alone. The proliferating possibilities that the future holds for these complex systems are discriminated from each other, not by differences of energy but by differences of dynamic structure. One catches the faintest glimmer of what might prove eventually to be a way of comprehending activity by both matter ("energy") and mind ("information") within a single metaphysical scheme.

The ontology modeled by the epistemology appropriate to chaos theory is therefore one in which holistic informational agencies can be at work within the supple confines of the physical world. I suggest that such active principles might take at least three forms:

1. There may be holistic laws of nature presently unknown

to us but capable of eventual scientific discovery. The amazing drive toward increasing complexification, discernible within the fruitful evolving history of the universe, may well require for its full understanding the operation of such laws.

2. As I have already suggested, here also may lie the eventual understanding of how human mental intention finds its realization within the flexible openness of our material bodies. It too is an expression of active information, though thought is very much more than the execution of information-processing algorithms.

3. It seems entirely possible that God also interacts with his creation through "information input" into its open physical process. Thus we glimpse in a rudimentary way what might lie behind the theological language, often associated with the work of the Spirit in Christian theology, of God's "guiding" and "drawing on" his creation, imminently working on the "inside" of cosmic process.

·

I believe that we can take with all seriousness all that science tells us about the workings of the world and still believe that the God who holds it in being has not left himself so impotent that he cannot continuously and consistently interact within cosmic history. Some consequences follow from this picture of the nature of divine action.

1. God's action will always be hidden. It will be contained within the cloudy unpredictabilities of what is going on. It may be discernible by faith, but it will not be exhibitable by experiment. It will more readily have the character of benign coincidence than of a naked act of power. It will be part of the complex nexus of occurrence from which it cannot be disentangled in some simplistic way that seeks to assert that God did this but nature did that. All forms of agency intertwine.

2. Although much of the physical world is cloudy, there are also clockwork parts of what is going on. Their regularity and predictability will be to the believer signs of divine faithfulness. Long ago, Origen recognized that one should not pray for

the cool of spring in the heat of summer (however tempting it might be to do so in his native Alexandria!). The succession of the seasons is a clockwork part of terrestrial experience, and the faithful God will not set that aside for the convenience of those who address him.

3. The picture I have given is of an open future in which both human and divine agency play parts in its accomplishment. Christian theology has, at its best, striven to find a way between two unacceptably extreme pictures of God's relationship to his creation. One is that of the cosmic tyrant who brings everything about by his will alone. He is the puppet-master of the universe, pulling every cosmic string and keeping all within his tight control. Such a God could not be the God of love, for the characteristic gift of love is of freedom to the beloved. In his action of creation, God has allowed the other truly to be, in the degree of independence appropriate to each part of it. As was discussed in chapter 5, an evolutionary universe is to be understood theologically as one that is allowed by God, within certain limits, to make itself. This gift of freedom is costly, for it carries with it the precariousness inherent in the self-restriction of divine control. Something relevant to the mystery of suffering is contained within this insight. I have already said that I believe that God wills neither the act of a murderer nor the incidence of a cancer, but God allows both to happen in a world that is permitted truly to be itself. But the God of love cannot be an indifferent spectator either. The detached God of deism, simply watching it all happen, is another extreme unacceptable to Christian thought. We seek a middle way in which God interacts with his creation without overruling it. There are many perplexities in trying to understand in any detail what this could mean. We encounter the cosmic version of the theological conundrum of the relation of divine grace to human free will.

4. It has sometimes been claimed that the view of God's action that I am advocating is a return to the discredited idea of a God of the Gaps. I deny that this is so in the pejorative sense

implied by the criticism. I am not invoking God to explain that which is currently scientifically unexplained, but which is, in principle, scientifically explicable. A God used to plug such gaps of ignorance is a pseudo-deity who will fade away with the advance of knowledge. Yet if there are indeed holistic causal principles (of any kind) at work in the world, there will have to be gaps in the bottom-up description that provide room for their operation. In this *intrinsic* sense, we are quite properly "people of the gaps" and God is quite properly a God of that kind of gap also.

5. I am developing a picture of a world of true becoming in which the dead hand of the Laplacean calculator is relaxed and the future is not a mere rearrangement of what was already there in the past. Such a genuinely temporal world must be known in its temporality, not least by God who knows things as they really are. If that is the case, there must be, as the process theologians have suggested, a temporal pole in the divine nature alongside the eternal pole recognized by classical theology. I also believe that in such a world even God does not know the future. That is no imperfection in the divine nature, for the unformed future is not yet there to be known. God possesses a current omniscience (God knows all that can now be known) but not a total omniscience (God does not yet know all that will be knowable). The act of creation involves a voluntary limitation, not only of divine power in allowing the other to be, but also of divine knowledge.

•

My belief is that we can take science with all seriousness, yet not conclude that the fabric of the physical world is so rigid in its structure that there cannot be powers of human and divine agency exercised within its unfolding history. Notice that I have been careful throughout to refer to God's *interaction*. I do so because I believe that God is continually and consistently related to the creation, and I eschew the word *intervention* because I believe that it carries overtones of the fitful and the arbitrary that are theologically unacceptable. The idea of a personal God exercising a special providence is not one that we have to give up. If that is the case, we can go on to inquire whether we can ask such a God to do particular things. In other words, what are we doing when we pray?

When the scientist prays, he or she knows that he or she has not been given a blank check on a heavenly account. There are great mysteries in the operation of divine providence. Not only are there the clashes of human desire — the vicar praying for a fine day for the church fete, the farmer praying for rain for his crops — but there are also the deeper strangenesses of individual human destiny. The English theologian Ian Ramsey told a story of two men crossing the plains of North America in a covered wagon in pioneer days. They are set upon by an Indian band, and a hail of arrows descends upon their vehicle. The horses are whipped up, and the two men make their escape. One of the men has survived the attack; his partner has been killed. Ramsey rightly says that if the survivor is to speak of God's providence in his survival, he must be prepared to speak also of God's providence in the death of his friend. There is no facile way of understanding these matters. After all, Christianity has a cross at the center of its story.

One might ask, Why do we have to pray at all? If God is good, will he not give us what is best for us without our having continually to ask for it? What is going on then when we pray? Are we persuading God to do something he would not bother to do if we did not make a fuss about it? Or are we drawing God's attention to something he might otherwise have forgotten? Or are we suggesting a rather clever plan that he had not thought of?

Obviously, none of these things can be right. I think, in fact, that we are doing two things when we pray:

1. My picture of how the future comes about is that we have some room for maneuver in its formation and that God has reserved to himself some room for providential maneuver also. I suggest that when we pray, we are offering our room for maneuver to be taken by God and used by him together with his

room for maneuver, to the greatest possible effect. Because I believe that there is an interconnectivity in things (holism again),
I believe that alignment can have consequences for third parties also. In more conventional language, we offer our wills to
be aligned with the divine will. A metaphor I often use is that
of laser light. What gives laser light its unusual effectiveness is
that it is what the physicists call "coherent." That means that
the waves making up the light are all in step. All the crests
come together and add up, and all the troughs come together
and add down, to the maximum effect. Light that is incoherent
has waves out of step; crests and troughs can coincide and can-
cel each other out. I believe that divine and human coherence
in prayer is genuinely instrumental; it can make things possible that would not be so if we and God were at cross-purposes.
Two consequences follow from this. One is that prayer is not a
substitute for action, but a spur to it. If my elderly neighbor is
tiresomely repetitious in the telling of the stories of his youth,
I do not absolve myself from the responsibility of patiently
listening yet again simply by praying for him. The second consequences of this picture of petitionary prayer is that it makes
sense of an intuition we have that corporate prayer is a good
idea — that it is appropriate to encourage many people to pray
for the same thing. This is not because there are more fists beat-
ing on the heavenly door, but because there are more wills to
be aligned with the divine will.

2. I owe the understanding of the second thing we are doing when we pray to some helpful thoughts of the Oxford
philosopher John Lucas. He says that when we pray we are
called upon to commit ourselves to what it is we really want;
in other words, to assign value. Such an assignment will be
taken seriously by God, though it is not, of course, an over-
riding obligation upon God, as if he were some heavenly Father
Christmas. When the blind man comes to Jesus in the Gospel
(Mark 10:46–52), the Lord says to him, "What do you want?"
It is perfectly clear what the man wants; he wants to regain his
sight. But he has to commit himself — to say, "Master, let me

receive my sight" — before he is healed. In a similar way, we have to say what it is we really wish for. I find that a helpful, if sobering, thought.

•

I hope that you will feel that the discourse of this chapter has been sober and reasonable. Of course, it has also been speculative, but in our present state of ignorance, no account of agency (whether human or divine) can avoid that being the case. I have tried in my thought to take both science and prayer seriously (as I do in my life) and to strive for a harmonious and integrated account. Yet you may feel that I have been dodging the main difficulty. It is all very well to talk of continuously acting divine providence hidden within the cloudy unpredictability of complex physical process, but does not religion trade in terms of shockingly discontinuous claims for divine intervention? Not to put too fine a point upon it, what about miracles? Are not these acts by their very definition *against* the grain of nature? Do we not here see the embarrassing and incredible spectacle of God conceived as acting like a celestial conjurer?

Etymologically, a miracle is something totally unexpected, something that evokes astonishment. A number of radically different kinds of events might be so classified. There might be the exercise of natural, but highly unusual or normally suppressed, powers of agency. A psychosomatic account of healing miracles would correspond to this idea. Some people do seem to have special healing gifts, and I am prepared to believe that Jesus possessed them pre-eminently. There might be significant coincidences (perhaps brought about by divine providence) of a kind that many of us feel we have experienced. It is possible to think of some of the nature miracles, like the stilling of the storm in the Gospels, in this way. These events might be called miraculous, but they easily fit into our earlier account, being understood as unexpected providences in unusual circumstances. But there remain radically unnatural claims, such as water into wine or making five loaves and two fishes feed thousands. Our assessment here is complicated by the fact that such incidents described in the Gospels carry a strong symbolic significance (the difference that Jesus makes), so that they might be inspirational stories that got into the record as if they were actual events. Christians will not all agree about how to assess these cases, but I cannot see that one could claim them as being central to Christian belief. What *is* central to such belief is the resurrection of Jesus on the first Easter day. Here we have the assertion of an event wholly contrary to natural expectation and experience, but one that any candid reading of the New Testament shows was an indispensable foundational belief of the early Christian movement. Do we face here an incredible belief in a celestial conjurer, or do we instead encounter an event wholly unexpected because it was possible only in a wholly unprecedented circumstance, an event that by its nature makes known a deeper level of divine consistency than had been revealed before? Delusion or deliverance? A mighty act of God or the creation of human wishful thinking? That is a vital question I will seek to answer in the next chapter.

- Seven -

RESURRECTION

THE COURSE of chapters 5 and 6 is a voyage inward toward the center. I started at the periphery with what was effectively natural theology — the attempt to see if our general knowledge of the universe, given us by science, may be construed as affording hints of a divine mind and purpose behind cosmic history. Such an investigation is a necessary part of the consonant harmonization of my experiences as a scientist and as a Christian believer. Then we drew nearer to the religious heart of things by seeking to investigate whether science's account of process, which must if it is to be satisfactory include space for the exercise of human agency, might not also be hospitable to divine providential interaction. Now I reach the point of encounter with what is the central ground of my own religious belief — the commanding, mysterious, but inescapable figure of Jesus Christ.

The instinct of a scientist is to look for the evidence that might motivate belief. We know that the world is full of surprises, so that confidence that we know beforehand what is reasonable and possible is strictly limited. Unprecedented or previously unexplored realms of experience may very well prove contrary in character to the familiar and the everyday. One has only to utter the words "quantum theory" to make the point. So the question the scientist wants to ask about belief —

including, of course, religious belief — is, What is it that makes you think this might be the case?

The reply to such an inquiry directed toward my own Christian belief would have to center on the figure of Jesus Christ. I learn about him from the tradition and teaching of the church, but the primary evidence must come from the New Testament, in particular, the Gospels. In assessing that evidence, I want to be scrupulous in taking advantage of critical historical inquiry, though a realistic assessment of the task will also recognize that there is no automatic or algorithmic procedure to which it can be reduced. In the end, tacit skills of judgment are called for concerning the relative credibilities of competing interpretations and the consequences of potentially obscuring and distorting effects — just as they are in science.

The question of Jesus is far too big a one to be addressed in a single chapter. Therefore I want to concentrate on what is, to my mind, the most important single issue. The founders of other great religious traditions — Moses, the Buddha, Muhammad — all die in honored old age, surrounded by their reverently attentive disciples. Jesus dies a painful and shameful death in early middle age, deserted by his frightened followers and with a cry of dereliction, "My God, my God, why have you forsaken me?" on his lips. The contrast is great. In that lonely and deserted figure hanging there on the cross, what do we see? A good man, like so many good men, both before and after him, finally caught and destroyed by the system? A man of megalomaniac pretension, who eventually got the comeuppance he deserved? Or, in the astonishing Christian claim, the Savior of the world? Only God can answer such a question. The earliest Christians believed that God had done so by raising Jesus from the dead. Is that a possible belief for us in the twentieth century?

The resurrection is the pivot on which Christian faith turns, and we have to explore whether the belief that God raised Jesus from the dead is one that is credible for us today. First one must look for historical evidence that might be held to motivate belief in so remarkable an occurrence. Yet how one actually weighs that evidence will be influenced by the extent to which we can make sense within a general worldview of the notion of the resurrection of Jesus. On its own terms, the resolute skepticism of a David Hume could never be overcome, whatever the quantity of evidence available. He has an unshakable certainty that "a miracle is a violation of the laws of nature; and as a firm and unalterable experience has established these laws, the proof against miracle, from the very nature of the fact, is as entire as any argument from experience can possibly be imagined." The confidence that the laws of nature were known with a certainty that extends even into realms of unprecedented and hitherto unexplored phenomena is one that was certainly falsified by the history of science subsequent to the eighteenth century. It could never be pressed to dispose of an event like the resurrection of Jesus, which claims to be a particular act of God in a unique circumstance.

If Jesus were just an ordinary wandering preacher, the chances are that, like all other men, he stayed dead; if he were more than that, then it is a coherent possibility that the aftermath of his death revealed new phenomena. Equally, if God raised him from the dead, that is surely a sign that he was indeed more than a wandering preacher. We cannot escape from that circularity. Neither can we escape from the insistent problem of how it came about that a man, living in a peripheral province of the Roman Empire, leaving virtually no trace in contemporary secular history, writing no book, dying a dismal death, nevertheless has been dominant in human life and thought ever since. "Who is Jesus?" and "Did God raise him?" are questions that inevitably interact. We must begin somewhere. I shall start with questions of evidence.

Something happened between Good Friday and Pentecost. The demoralization of the disciples, caused by the arrest and execution of their Master is certain. Equally certain is the fact that within a short space of time, those same disciples were defying the authorities, who had previously seemed so threatening, and were proclaiming the one who had died disgraced and forsaken as being both Lord and Christ. If that had not happened, there would have been no Christian movement. So great a transformation calls for an equally great cause. From the nineteenth century onward, it has been suggested that what happened was a faith event in the minds of the disciples, a conviction achieved after a period of reflection, so that the cause of Jesus continued beyond his death. That does not seem to me to begin to be sufficiently powerful enough to be the explanation of so great a transformation.

Even less likely is the theory, first suggested in the nineteenth century and still occasionally put forward, that Jesus swooned on the cross and revived in the cool of the tomb. In addition to the many historical implausibilities involved, this idea fails to convince because, as David Strauss rightly emphasized, a half-dead figure could not have given the impression he had conquered death. However, Strauss believed it was a hallucinatory experience that could have been the trigger of the change in the disciples' attitude. The remorse of Peter caused in him a reaction which then communicated itself to the fraught band of disciples in a psychological chain reaction. Such an explanation fails to account for the varieties of time and place associated in the tradition with the claimed appearances, including Paul's experience on the Damascus road, which must have been three years or so after the crucifixion. It also makes a good number of unsubstantiated assumptions about the temperamental makeup of the disciples. In any case, surely hallucinations, however vivid, could not have been the enduring basis of the vitality of the early Christian movement.

The New Testament answer to what happened is that Jesus had been raised from the dead and that he showed himself to his disciples. It is important to remember that the earliest account of the resurrection appearances does not occur in the Gospels but in Paul's first letter to the Corinthians, written in the middle fifties AD. Paul had founded the Corinthian church, and he reminds them of the following:

I delivered to you as of first importance what I also received, that Christ died for our sins in accordance with the
scriptures, that he was buried, that he was raised on the
third day in accordance with the scriptures, and that he
appeared to Cephas, then to the twelve. Then he appeared
to more than five hundred brethren at one time, most of
whom are still alive, though some have fallen asleep. Then
he appeared to James, then to all the apostles. Last of all,
as to one untimely born, he appeared also to me. (1 Cor.
15:3–8)

When Paul says he delivered what he also received, we must
surely suppose that he is referring to teaching given immediately following his conversion, just a few years after the
crucifixion itself. Thus this testimony takes us back very close
indeed to the events cited. The antiquity of the material is confirmed by the use of the Aramaic "Cephas" for Peter and by
the reference to "the twelve," a phrase that soon fell out of
Christian usage. The style of the reference to the five hundred
brethren makes it plain that an appeal to accessible testimony is
being made. It is entirely possible that this attestatory role is the
reason why there is no reference in Paul's list to the witness of
the women (prominent in the Gospel accounts of appearances),
because in the ancient male-dominated world their testimony
would not have been acceptable.

The account in 1 Corinthians 15 is extremely short, a simple list of witnesses. It concludes with Paul's own encounter
with the risen Christ, referred to again by the apostle himself in
Galatians and three times described in Acts. One might suppose
Paul's experience to be that of a vision; but if so, vision is used
in a distinctive sense, for elsewhere the New Testament proves
perfectly capable of speaking of visionary experience in terms
carrying much less significance than is attached to the case of
the resurrection appearances (e.g., Acts 23:11). Paul's Damascus
road encounter is special and it is the ground of his apostleship.
It is critical for his authority that he should find a place in that

list of witnesses, alongside Peter and James and the rest. So we must suppose his experience was comparable to theirs. To assess what that might be we have to turn to what the Gospels can tell us.

Immediately one enters a strange, almost dreamlike world in which Jesus appears in rooms with locked doors and suddenly disappears again. There is considerable difference of account among the different Gospels. This latter point is in marked contrast to the preceding stories of the Passion. These certainly display variations of detail, but they are plainly recounting the same broad sequence of events. The Gospel treatments of the resurrection appearances are much more diverse.

Matthew records a meeting of the risen Jesus with the women (Matt. 28:9–10), at which he tells them he will meet his "brethren" in Galilee, and subsequently such a meeting is described (Matt. 28:16–20). The account of the latter includes a Trinitarian formula that must surely be a quite late development in the tradition.

Mark, at least as far as the authentic text available to us is concerned, does not give a description of any appearance of the risen Jesus, though one is foreshadowed in 16:7: "He is going before you to Galilee; there you will see him, as he told you." Scholars have argued whether there is a lost conclusion to the Gospel that would have supplied the present lack. Our text ends with the words about the women at the tomb: "They said nothing to any one, for they were afraid" (Mark 16:8). However much it might suit modern taste to end in mystery and fear, I greatly doubt whether a first-century writer would have seen it that way. By the second century it was felt appropriate to construct the additions to Mark that figure in some manuscripts and many of our versions. These incorporate ancient tradition, but they cannot be considered to be an independent witness in relation to the other Gospels.

In Luke 24 everything happens in Jerusalem on the first Easter day itself. Jesus does not meet with the women, but he journeys to Emmaus with two of the disciples. He later appears to the assembled eleven, finally parting from them after he has led them out to Bethany. There is also a brief reference to an appearance to Peter. The same author in Acts speaks in general terms of appearances stretching over a period of forty days.

The most extensive sequence of resurrection appearances is described in John. Jesus is seen by Mary Magdalene (John 20:11–18). Then he appears to the eleven less Thomas on Easter evening, and a week later again to them all, including Thomas this time, who exclaims, "My Lord and My God!" (John 20:19–29). In what appears to be an appendix added to the Gospel, we are given the detailed story of an appearance by the lakeside in Galilee (John 21:1–23).

It is a somewhat confusing mass of material. Yet amid the variety of the appearance stories there is one element that is both unexpected and persistent. It is that it was difficult to *recognize* the risen Jesus. Mary Magdalene mistakes Jesus for the gardener; on the Lake of Galilee, only the beloved disciple has the insight to recognize that the figure on the shore is the Lord; the couple walking to Emmaus realize who their companion has been only at the moment of the breaking of bread and his disappearance; with great frankness Matthew tells us that when Jesus appeared on the mountain in Galilee "they worshiped him; but some doubted" (Matt. 28:17). This would be an odd motif to recur in stories that were merely made up. It seems likely to me that, on the contrary, it is a genuine historical reminiscence.

It is important to recognize that the Gospel accounts of the resurrection of Jesus are not telling the story of a resuscitated corpse. Whatever we may make of the stories of those whom Jesus restored to life, there can be no question that they were destined eventually to die again. They were resuscitated, not resurrected. Jesus, however, is raised to endless life; his resurrection body is transmuted and glorified, possessing the unprecedented properties that allow him to appear and disappear in locked rooms, yet bearing still the scars of the Passion.

It is now necessary to consider a second line of evidence that has a potential bearing on these questions. I refer to the stories of the empty tomb. All four Gospels contain accounts of how, once the Sabbath was over, women came to the tomb to attend to the body of Jesus, only to find the stone rolled away and the tomb empty (Mark 16:1-8). These stories differ in details, but that need not disconcert us. We can accept such variation without believing that this by itself casts doubt on the core tradition. Anyone familiar with evidence being given in the police courts will recognize that witnesses will differ on various points, while still obviously describing the same incident.

Are these stories, as some believe, the strongest evidence for the resurrection? Why did the Jerusalem authorities not nip the nascent Christian movement in the bud by exhibiting the moldering body of its leader? It is surely incredible to suggest that the disciples stole the body in an act of contrived deceit, and unbelievably lame to suggest that the women went to the wrong tomb. The only credible reason for the emptiness of the sepulchre was that Jesus had actually risen. So the argument goes.

In fact, however, we must be a bit more careful. The first explicit account of the empty tomb is in Mark, written some thirty-five years or so after the event. Could this be a second-generation story, made up as the expression of an already existing conviction (perhaps based on the appearances) that Jesus had survived death? Even the fact of a distinct tomb at all is held to be questionable, for it was the common Roman practice to inter executed felons in the anonymity of a common grave. A number of points may be made in reply.

While it is well known that Paul does not refer explicitly to the empty tomb in his extant letters, not only is the argument from silence particularly dangerous when applied to such unsystematic writings, but also the occurrence of the phrase "was buried" in that extraordinarily brief summary in 1 Corinthians 15 seems clearly to indicate that a special significance was attached to the burial of Jesus. It seems hard to believe that a Jew like Paul, whose background of thought would have emphasized the psychosomatic unity of the human being, could have believed that Jesus was alive but that his tomb still contained his moldering body.

If it were a made-up story, it is hard to see why Joseph of Arimathea and Nicodemus are the names associated with it, for these figures do not play any prominent part in the subsequent story of the Christian movement. The most natural explanation of their assignment to an honored role is that they fulfilled it.

Equally, if the discovery of the empty tomb were a made-up story, why, in the male-dominated world of that time, were Mary Magdalene and the other women chosen to play the key parts? Far and away the most natural answer is that they actually did so. Of course, there are oddities about the story. How did the women imagine they were going to cope with the heavy stone blocking the entrance? (This problem is acknowledged in Mark 16:3.) After three days, in that hot climate, would it not have been too late to attend to the corpse? However, Jewish tradition held that corruption set in on the fourth day, and John (John 19:39–40) suggests that some preliminary precautions had been taken on the Friday evening. Such problems are, perhaps, more characteristic of the roughness of real memories than concocted stories, and, in any case, one should not expect coolly logical behavior from women still upset at the execution of their revered Master.

In any case, these difficulties do not seem to have been shared by critics of Christianity in the ancient world. As a bitter polemical argument sprang up between Jews and Christians, it was always accepted that there was a tomb and that it was empty. The critical counter-suggestion was that the disciples had stolen the body in an act of deception, an explanation that I regard as incredible. Just how far back this argument can be traced is indicated by the story of the watch set on the tomb (Matt. 27:62–66; 28:11–15). This must be a fabricated tale from a Christian source, concocted precisely to rebut the rumor that the disciples had been graverobbing. Thus there is clear evidence that in the first century those hostile to Christianity accepted that the tomb had been found empty. Yet contrary to some modern apologists, the Gospels do not present the empty tomb as a knockdown argument for the truth of the resurrection. Rather, it requires explanation. Hence the need for the message of the angel: "He has risen; he is not here" (Mark 16:6, par.). In the story of Peter and the beloved disciple at the tomb (John 20:3–10), it is only the latter who has the insight to recognize unaided what has happened. For the others, the discovery of the emptiness of the tomb is, at first, upsetting. There is no easy triumphalism in these stories, which itself makes one the more inclined to accept them as stemming from authentic recollection. From the point of view of the New Testament, it is the resurrection that explains the empty tomb rather than the empty tomb proving the resurrection.

It is interesting that there are twentieth-century Jewish writers who accept the emptiness of the tomb without thereby being driven to embrace Christianity. Geza Vermes concludes: "In the end, when every argument has been considered and weighed, the only conclusion acceptable to the historian must be... that the women who set out to pay their last respects to Jesus found to their consternation, not a body, but an empty tomb." The orthodox Jew Pinchas Lapide goes further. He believes that Jesus was raised from the dead, but he does not accept him as the Messiah, He writes that "according to my opinion, the resurrection belongs to the category of the truly real and effective occurrences, for without a fact of history there is no act of true faith."

In the meantime, let us add to the circumstantial discussion of the traditions of the appearances and the empty tomb certain other inferential considerations that have a bearing on the resurrection. Why is Sunday, the first day of the week, the special Christian day, despite the church's origin in a Jewish setting for which the Sabbath, the seventh day, was the day of special religious significance? The answer is that, from the earliest Christian times, Sunday has been the Lord's day, the day of resurrection. It is the "third day" from Good Friday, mentioned in the primitive teaching.

Strictly speaking, the third day is preserved as the day on which the tomb was found empty and the Lord first appeared to his disciples. There is an impressive discretion in the Gospels that restrains them from any attempt to describe God's act of resurrection itself. The well-known passage in the apocryphal Gospel of Peter shows us how inadequate pious fancy proved for this task when second-century curiosity encouraged the concoction of such descriptions.

A final consideration is one that the nonbeliever may treat with some reserve but one that is unquestionably part of the Christian witness. The church in every century has characteristically spoken of Jesus as its living Lord in the present; it does not look back to him as a revered founder-figure of the past. The church is like the "background radiation" persisting after the primary event of the raising of Jesus. Its fundamental claim is "Jesus lives!" There is a great contrast here with the other great religious traditions of the world, which do not speak of their revered founders in such contemporary terms.

There is also a striking contrast between the early Christian assertion that a recently known figure was resurrected within history and the contemporary expectations of the ancient world. Many, but not all, Jews looked for a general resurrection of the dead at the end of time. It was a different thing altogether for a resurrection to take place *within* history. Hence the initial consternation at its discovery. The embarrassing scene in Matthew, where the death of Jesus provokes an earthquake and the saints come out of their tombs (Matt. 27:51–54), is precisely an attempt in pictorial language to associate with Jesus within history those eschatological events that really belong beyond history, in the effort to cope with the perplexity involved in his *historical* resurrection. Comparisons with Egyptian stories about Isis or Greek stories about Aesculapius miss the point that these refer to legendary figures of the mythological past, not to a wandering preacher who but yesterday was drawing the crowds.

I hope I have made it clear that there is motivation for the belief that Jesus was raised from the dead (the most ancient expression is always in the passive; it is a great act of God, not a final miracle of Jesus, which is being asserted). We now have to ask the question whether the motivation provided is in fact strong enough to support the extraordinary claim being made. Such an assessment will depend upon whether it makes sense within a general understanding of God and his ways with humanity that alone of all who have ever lived, this man was restored to unending life in an act that, although it transcends history, nevertheless is embedded in history.

Inevitably we return to the way in which the significance of Jesus and the truth of his resurrection inevitably interact. Is there about him something that made it fitting that God should raise him from the dead? Did his life end in failure, or was he vindicated after death? Yet the resurrection, if it happened, would be not only the vindication of Jesus. It would also be the vindication of God — that God did not abandon the one man who wholly trusted himself to him. Moreover, we begin to see here some glimmer of a divine response to the problem of evil. If Good Friday testifies to the reality of the power of evil, Easter Day shows that the last word lies with God.

Finally, the resurrection of Jesus is the vindication of our human hopes. We will all die with our lives to a greater or lesser extent incomplete, unfulfilled, unhealed. Yet there is a profound and widespread human intuition that in the end all will be well. As someone once said, there is a wistful longing that the murderer should not triumph over his innocent victim. The resurrection of Jesus is the sign that such human hope is not delusory. It is part of Christian understanding that what happened to Jesus within history is a foretaste and guarantee of what will await all of us beyond history. "For as in Adam all die, so also in Christ shall all be made alive" (1 Cor. 15:22). All these considerations indicate to me that the resurrection of Jesus makes sense. It fits in with who he was, and who God is, and who we are.

In Christian understanding, the resurrection of Jesus is a

great act of God; but its singularity is its timing, not its nature, for it is an historical anticipation of the eschatological destiny of the whole of humankind. The resurrection is the beginning of God's great act of redemptive transformation, the seed from which the new creation begins to grow (cf. 2 Cor. 5:17). When Jesus himself was questioned by the Sadducees about the idea of a general resurrection at the end of time, he based his answer on the faithfulness of God, the God for whom Abraham, Isaac, and Jacob were not simply persons who had served their turn and then were discarded, but they were people of continuing significance to him (Mark 12:18–27, par.).

That, in a nutshell, is the case for the fittingness of a belief in the resurrection of Jesus as well as the belief in a destiny for ourselves in him.

When I first wrote about these matters, I concluded that when we consider the New Testament evidence

> the only explanation which is commensurate with the phenomena is that Jesus rose from the dead in such a fashion (whatever that may be) that it is true to say that he is alive today, glorified and exalted but still continuously related in a mysterious but real way with the historical figure who lived and died in first-century Palestine.

I stand by that judgment today.

– Eight –

THE END
OF ALL THINGS

Then I saw a new heaven and a new earth; for the first
heaven and the first earth had passed away, and the sea was
no more.

— Revelation 21:1

When cosmologists think about the ultimate fate of the universe, they conclude that it is going to end badly. A gigantic
tug-of-war is going on between two opposing cosmic principles.
One is the expansive force of the Big Bang, blowing the galaxies apart. The other is the contractive force of gravity, pulling
them together. These two tendencies are almost in balance, and
we cannot tell which will gain the ultimate upper hand. If expansion eventually prevails, the galaxies will continue to recede
from each other forever. Within each galaxy, however, gravity
will certainly win, and the galaxies will condense into gigantic
black holes that will in time decay into low-grade radiation. If
that is the future scenario, the universe will end in a whimper.
The prospect is no less bleak if gravity prevails. In that case, the
present expansion will one day be halted and reversed. What
began with the Big Bang will end in the Big Crunch, as the

whole world falls back into a cosmic melting pot. That way, the universe ends in a bang. Either way, it is condemned to futility.

These prognostications of the end of present physical process deserve to be taken with the utmost seriousness. It will not happen tomorrow. Tens of billions of years of cosmic history lie ahead. But it is as certain as can be that humanity will prove to be a transient episode in that history. "Vanity, vanity, all is vanity," said the Preacher. Science shows us that this is indeed so, and theology must be prepared to take that seriously. Here is a challenge to the claim that a will lies behind cosmic process, that a purpose is being worked out in the history of the universe. In the early years of this century Bertrand Russell wrote, "Only within the scaffolding of these truths, only on the firm foundation of unyielding despair, can the soul's habitation henceforth be safely built."

I agree with the first of these provisos, but not the second. For the Christian, in the end is neither a bang nor a whimper but the eternal faithfulness of God. Our religion has never subscribed to an evolutionary optimism, expecting the kingdom of God to find its complete fulfillment within present history. I do not think that the death of the universe, on a timescale of tens of billions of years, poses problems altogether different from the knowledge of our even more certain deaths, on a timescale of tens of years. We hope for a destiny beyond death for ourselves. Because the whole of the creation matters to God — this vast universe is not here just to be the backdrop for the human drama being played out on a speck of cosmic dust after an overture lasting fifteen billion years — it too must have an everlasting destiny within God's faithful purposes. The argument for that is the same as that which Jesus used in his dispute with the Sadducees. The God of Abraham, Isaac, and Jacob is "not God of the dead, but of the living" (Mark 12:27). The patriarchs were not people who had served their purpose and were then discarded. Because they mattered to God once, they matter to him forever. In God *all* that is good has an everlasting hope. No good will be lost.

Eschatology is not a speculative optional extra for Christianity. It is central to a credible theology. Without an everlasting hope, present hope is no more than a device to endure this world's ambiguity. Defiance of futility would be a more noble stance if there were indeed no prospect beyond the grave, for us or for the universe. But there is such a hope. "Then I saw a new heaven and a new earth; for the first heaven and the first earth had passed away, and the sea was no more." An immense divine redemptive act of cosmic scope is here set before us. What ends in corruption will be raised in immortality. We have emerged from the universe in the course of its fruitful evolutionary history, and in some appropriate but unimaginable way it will share with us in the new life of Christ's eternal kingdom. Our personal hope is not survival, but resurrection, the re-embodied destiny that is the coherent and credible aspiration for psychosomatic unities like ourselves. The "real me" is not a spiritual ghost hidden within the discardable material husk of my body. We are not apprentice angels. The "real me" is the almost infinitely complex information-bearing pattern that persists through the continuously changing flux of atoms through my body. The soul is the form of that body, a thought that would not have surprised Thomas Aquinas. The pattern that is me is dissolved at death, but it is a coherent hope that it will be remembered by God and reconstituted by him in his great act of resurrection. That re-embodiment will surely be in the transmuted environment that is the redeemed universe, the new heaven and the new earth.

We are told of this new creation that "the sea was no more." Our British and American seafaring races might regret that, but to the Hebrew the sea was the waters of chaos, the symbol of all that is life-threatening. The new creation is not going to be just a rerun of the old. It will be redeemed from both present and future futility and frustration. "He will wipe away every tear from their eyes, and death shall be no more, neither shall there be mourning nor crying nor pain any more, for the former things have passed away" (Rev. 21:4).

It is a wonderful vision. But is it a coherent possibility? The difficulty is this. In our present world, change and decay are built into the fabric of the universe. The processes by which genetic mutations produce new forms of life are the processes by which cells become cancerous. Death is the necessary cost of life. In fact, a theological defense of the existence of physical evil is that it is not gratuitous but the inescapable price of an evolutionary world, free to make itself within the independence its Creator has granted to it. I have elsewhere called this the free-process defense. If that picture is correct, how can the new creation be so very different? And if it can — if its "matter" can be subject to physical laws different from ours and free from inbuilt transience — why did not the Creator bring into being a world like that in the first instance, instead of this flawed and costly universe? To put it bluntly, if the new creation is going to be so wonderful, why did God bother with the old?

It is a serious question. The answer lies, I think, in a just recognition of the character of the new creation. It is not a second attempt by God to do better than he had managed to do the first time around. It is not a *second* creation but a truly *new* creation, one moreover that could come about only by the redemption of the old creation. The first creation was *ex nihilo*. It was God's bringing about, in his freedom and his love, the existence of something other than himself. God made way for it, over against himself. It was endowed with potential fruitfulness by its Creator — as the scientific insights of the anthropic principle quite astonishingly testify; but then it was allowed, in its evolutionary history, to make itself. It was not outside God's providential care, but it was released from his tight control. Every parent knows that the gift of love must include the costly and precarious gift of independence to the beloved.

The laws of nature of that first creation were those that were appropriate to such a world, allowed to realize its own potentiality. The new creation will be something different; it is a creation *ex vetere*, for it is the transmutation of the old *consequent upon its free return to its Creator.* I struggle to grasp that deeply mys-

terious notion, but I am sure that it is central to a consistent
and convincing eschatology. Although the world was created as
other than God, its final fulfillment is not to stand alone but
to be reunited freely with the life of its Creator. We know that
for ourselves; it is God's service that will be our perfect freedom. In a strange but appropriate way it will be so for all that
God has made. I am stutteringly trying to articulate what our
Eastern Orthodox friends have long spoken about in terms of
theosis, the cosmic destiny in which God will be all in all, in
which God's life will suffuse all that is. I do not accept panen-
theism — that the world is part of God — as a present reality,
but I do embrace it as the hope of our ultimate destiny. What
is not possible in terms of the abolition of pain and transience
while the creation is separated from its Creator can be possible
through its full return to God in Christ. There are hints of this
in scripture: in Paul's amazing vision in Romans 8 of a creation
"subjected to futility: that will obtain "the glorious liberty of
the children of God" (vv. 20–21); and above all in the figure of
the Cosmic Christ of Colossians 1 in whom "all the fulness of
God was pleased to dwell, and through him to reconcile to himself all things (*ta panta*), whether on earth or in heaven, making
peace by the blood of his cross" (Col. 1:19–20). There are also
hints of this in experience, particularly in the Real Presence in
the sacrament. The ultimate destiny of the whole universe is
sacramental. What is now known locally and occasionally will
then be known globally and forever.

The seed from which the new creation grows has already
been sown, for it is the resurrection of Christ that is the seminal
event. That is why I believe that the empty tomb is so important for Christian theology. It tells us that the Lord's risen and
glorified body is the transmuted form of his dead body. The
latter is not discarded as a husk that has served its purpose; it
shares in the resurrection life. That speaks to us of a destiny for
matter in Christ, as well as a destiny for humanity. We must be
careful not to be too purely spiritually minded.

Eschatology may seem to be a curious subject for a theologically minded scientist to have chosen, but we need to embrace the Advent hope. I believe that the interaction between science and theology is deep and interpenetrating, and that it is not confined simply to boundary topics such as natural theology, however important these may be. If we take our knowledge of transience seriously, it will provoke us to ask how we may take our deep intuition of hope equally seriously. It is important that the church does not lose its nerve in talking about a destiny beyond death, whether that death is our own or the universe's. In speaking of that destiny, we are not invoking pie-in-the-sky but are addressing an issue without which Christian theology is incomplete and unconvincing. The great vision of the Seer of Patmos of a new heaven and a new earth is an essential part of Christian hope and Christian belief. Now to the one true God, who will wipe away every tear from our eyes, to Father, Son, and Holy Spirit, be all might, majesty, dominion, and praise, now and forever. Amen.

– Conclusion –

TAKING REALITY SERIOUSLY

SCIENCE is wonderfully successful precisely because it limits itself to certain types of questions (essentially, How?) and draws upon a certain impersonal kind of experience (essentially, the world treated as "it," as an object). We should take science absolutely seriously, but it would be grotesque to suppose that science was the only form of inquiry into reality worthy of our attention. Science deliberately leaves out of its account questions of meaning, purpose, and value, and it disregards all that great swath of personal experience and encounter that actually constitutes most of what makes life worth living. We need a wider view. Music is more than vibrating air. Our belief that love is better than hate is true knowledge. I also believe that the Christian claim that God has made himself known in the plainest possible terms through the life, death, and resurrection of Jesus Christ is the most important and most exciting insight possible into the nature of reality.

The chapters that constitute this volume are based on two fundamental convictions. First, our view of reality should aim to be as comprehensive as possible. We live in a many-layered world that is not only orderly and fertile in the way that science discovers, but is also the carrier of beauty, the arena of moral decision, and the place of encounter with the presence of God. I am a passionate believer in the unity of knowledge. Science and religion need each other, and that is why they must talk to each other and why their conversation will bear fruit for both parties. Second, the key to all understanding, in science, religion, or other forms of inquiry, is the search for motivated belief, pursued with imaginative daring. Religion does not trade in unquestionable certainties that have to be accepted by the faithful because they are endowed with an unchallengeable authority. Christian believers are called to give a *reason* for the hope that is in them (1 Pet. 3:15).

I have tried to indicate how these twin convictions work out for me as a physicist who is also a priest. I am convinced that the survival of Christianity in a scientific age does not call for watering down the faith, so that God becomes simply the cosmic architect and Jesus an inspiring figure of the past. Scientists know that the world is strange and exciting, beyond our power to anticipate before we encounter its surprising nature. The religion of the Incarnation is mysterious and counter to our everyday intuition, just as the quantum world is contrary to Newtonian expectation. We can see neither God nor electrons, but both make sense of the richness of reality. If I can persuade some of my readers to take both seriously, I shall be well content.

NOTES

One: Christian Belief in a Scientific Age

1. Bernard Lonergan, *Insight* (Longman, 1957), 684.

Three: Taking Science Seriously

1. See J. C. Polkinghorne, *Rochester Roundabout* (W. H. Freeman, 1989), chap. 21; also idem, *One World* (Princeton, N.J.: Princeton University Press, 1986), and *Reason and Reality* (Trinity Press International, 1991).
2. M. Polanyi, *Personal Knowledge* (Routledge & Kegan Paul, 1958).
3. J. Leslie, *Universes* (Routledge & Kegan Paul, 1989).
4. J. Gleick, *Chaos* (William Heinemann, 1988).
5. Polkinghorne, *Reason and Reality*, chap. 3.
6. J. C. Polkinghorne, *The Quantum World* (Princeton University Press, 1984), chap. 6.
7. See W. H. Vanstone, *Love's Endeavour, Love's Expense* (Darton, Longman & Todd, 1977).

Four: Taking Theology Seriously

1. I. G. Barbour, *Religion in an Age of Science* (Harper & Row, 1990); A. R. Peacocke, *Intimations of Reality* (University of Notre Dame Press, 1984); J. C. Polkinghorne, *Reason and Reality* (Trinity Press International, 1991), chaps. 1 and 2.
2. B. Lonergan, *Insight* (Longman, 1957), 684.
3. J. C. Polkinghorne, *Science and Providence* (Shambhala, 1989), chap. 5.
4. J. Moltmann, *The Crucified God* (SCM Press, 1974).

INDEX